SCOTCH PASSION

An Anthology of
Scottish Erotic Poetry

BOOKS BY ALEXANDER SCOTT

Poetry

The Latest in Elegies
Selected Poems
Untrue Thomas
Mouth Music
Cantrips
Greek Fire
Double Agent
Selected Poems 1943–1974

Prose

Still Life: William Soutar 1898–1943
The MacDiarmid Makars

Edited

William Jeffrey: Selected Poems
Alexander Scott: The Poems
William Soutar: Diaries of a Dying Man
Contemporary Scottish Verse (with Norman MacCaig)
The Hugh MacDiarmid Anthology (with Michael Grieve)
Neil M. Gunn: The Man and the Writer (with Douglas Gifford)
Scottish Poetry 7–9 (with Maurice Lindsay and Roderick Watson)
Modern Scots Verse 1922–1977

SCOTCH PASSION

*An Anthology of
Scottish Erotic Poetry*

compiled by
Alexander Scott

ROBERT HALE · LONDON

ISBN 0 7091 9884 1

Robert Hale Limited
Clerkenwell House
Clerkenwell Green
London EC1R 0HT

Photoset in Palatino by
Kelly Typesetting Limited
Bradford-on-Avon, Wiltshire
Printed in Great Britain by
St Edmundsbury Press
Bury St Edmunds, Suffolk
Bound by Hunter & Foulis Limited

To
CATHERINE
but for whom . . .

Contents

Contents

Note: Where an asterisk appears after the title of a poem, a note will be found in the section beginning on page 197.

Acknowledgements

For permission to use copyright poems I am obliged to J. K. Annand and Macdonald Publishers; David Black; Alan Bold; Tom Buchan; the Estate of Robert Garioch and Carcanet Press; Valerie Gillies and Canongate; the Estate of Sir Alexander Gray; Andrew Greig; Robin Hamilton; Alan Jackson; William Keys; John Kincaid; T. S. Law; Tom Leonard; Maurice Lindsay and Paul Harris Publishing; Liz Lochhead and Next Editions; Norman MacCaig and Hogarth Press Ltd; Mrs Valda Grieve and Martin Brian and O'Keeffe Ltd, for poems by Hugh MacDiarmid; Alastair Mackie; Edwin Morgan and Ian McKelvie for 'Campobasso Italy Undated Reported March 1971'; Edwin Morgan and Edinburgh University Press for 'From a City Balcony'; Edwin Morgan and Carcanet Press for his other poems; the Estate of Edwin Muir and Faber and Faber Ltd; Akros Publications for poems by Alexander Scott; Mrs Hazel Smith and John Calder Ltd, for poems by Sydney Goodsir Smith; The National Library of Scotland for poems by William Soutar; the Estate of Muriel Stuart; William J. Tait and Paul Harris Publishing; W. Price Turner.

Introduction

Scottish poetry—as distinct from patriotic song and verse-romance—begins in passion, early in the fifteenth century, and has remained involved with the erotic throughout all the revolutions in church and state of some six hundred years. Such a statement may come as a surprise, even as a shock, to those whose image of the Scot is the stereotype of the hard-headed expatriate go-getter whose only emotional release from money-making is excessively expressed in the self-flagellation of religious puritanism or in the alcoholic sentimentalities of an uncreative chauvinism (or both), but it is one of the purposes of the following pages to transform the astonishment of such readers into "the shock of recognition". Scottish poets have never conformed to the conventional caricature where Calvinism is the grim bed-fellow of commerce, and the heads on their pillows present an altogether more animating and attractive picture.

Among our many poets of passion, who include well-nigh all of our major makars, the earliest is a prince, King James I of Scotland (1394–1437), the most famous a ploughman, Robert Burns (1759–1796). Others have been lairds, lawyers, professors, priests, civil servants, schoolteachers, administrators, artists, housewives, hacks, miners, musicians, farmers and philosophers. Yet others, authors of ballads and folk-songs which circulated orally for a debatable number of centuries, are unidentifiable among the great mass of those local communities of the people for whom they composed. The passion which all of them have experienced and expressed is a moving force at every level of our society, as in every age of our history, whether radical or repressive.

The great hymn in praise of Eros which opens our account of this long *affaire de passion*, James I's *The Kingis Quair*, is the finest extended love-poem written in this island before renaissance and reformation irrevocably altered the intellectual and imaginative landscape in which the unchanging emotions operate. Superbly expressing adoration of the beloved, the *Quair* is equally superb in its realisation of physical desire, its presentation of the lady as a creature of flesh and blood whose beauty stimulates the lover's senses as well as his willingness to worship at Love's shrine. At the same time, however, the poem is a work of high—or, at least, respectable—morality, discussing and distinguishing the differences between "lawful" and "unlawful" love and advancing arguments in favour of Christian marriage which are diametrically opposed to the glorifications of adultery in which so much earlier medieval love-poetry engages. Since those arguments are quite devoid of erotic feeling, the passages in which they are expressed have not been included here, but the distinction that they draw between the legal and the illicit, the hallowed and the unholy, is one that appears to have haunted the minds of many Scottish poets for as long as religion remained a dominant social and intellectual force.

A seminal work, *The Kingis Quair* anticipates some major themes of many later Scottish erotic poems. In the love-poetry of its royal author's immediate successor, the scholar-schoolmaster Robert Henryson (*c.* 1420–*c.* 1490), who was a priest in minor orders, the adulterous passion enjoined by the medieval code of love is either mocked, as in the ironical pastoral comedy 'Robene and Makyne', or condemned to ruin, as in the greatest of all Scottish verse-tragedies, 'The Testament of Cresseid'. But whether Henryson laughs at, or mourns over, the frustrations of his lovers, his keen awareness of the sensuous fascination of Eros thrills throughout his lines, even while the erotic passion he delineates is either decried or denied. His synthesis of attraction and repulsion has been echoed by a long line of distinguished later poets, from Sir George Clapperton (*c.* 1505–1574) and the first Alexander Scott (*c.* 1515–*c.* 1583)— whose distrust of promiscuous sex may have been deepened by their involvement in Scotland's Calvinist reformation in the 1560s—to one of our own younger contemporaries, Liz Lochhead (b. 1948), whose 'Song of Solomon' analyses the relationship of disgust to desire with a delicate female wit which is as scintillating as it is subtle. Even Sir Walter Scott (1771–1832), whose verse and prose alike are usually so empty of eroticism that he has come to be regarded as The Greatest Bore of All Time by those awakening adolescents on whom his "safely" sexless pages are inflicted in the schoolroom, has produced a poem in this mode which is a brilliantly incisive exception to his all too arid rule. Among numerous modern poets, the most dramatic, and the most widely-ranging in this genre is Edwin Morgan (b. 1920), whose evocations of the destructive power of desire are etched in the starkest lines as if by the most corrosive acid manipulated by the most cunning of burned fingers.

Henryson's younger contemporary, William Dunbar (*c.* 1465–*c.* 1513), an unbeneficed cleric, is more critically concerned than his predecessor with the unsatisfactory social conditions which have resulted in the exploitation, and consequent coarsening, of the erotic. His *The Tretis of the Tua Marriit Wemen and the Wedo* is still the greatest extended satire of degraded sexuality in Scottish verse. Yet the sensuous impact of the writing in this poem provides almost overwhelming evidence of the power which sexual pleasure exercises over men and women, creating a tension between dislike and desire that vibrates through every line. In Dunbar it is the marriage customs of his time which have turned his "fair ladies" into wantons, whereas in Allan Ramsay (1686–1758) and Sydney Goodsir Smith (1915–1975) that wantonness has become a profession. Ramsay's 'Lucky Spence's Last Advice', where an old procuress defiantly defends her trade, provides shrewd—if oblique—satire of the society that has created the demand for which that traffic caters, while Goodsir Smith's 'Nicht o Lust' first erects, and finally demolishes, the romantic view of the whore as The Great Release. Extracted from Elegy XIII of Goodsir Smith's masterpiece, *Under the Eildon Tree* (1948; revised edition 1954), an extended study of the pursuit of love (and lust), 'Nicht o Lust' is at once the centre, and the poetic climax, of the whole work, interweaving romantic fantasy with sharp-eyed factual satire both of society and of the poet himself in a vivid tapestry of passion's paradoxical power at once to attract and repel. While *Under the Eildon Tree* remains unmatched in Scottish poetry for the range of its exploration of the myriad facets of sexual love, the extensions of commercialised sex in the decades since it was first published have attracted the attentions of yet younger poets, in whose work the struggle between fascination and contempt is variously poised but always potent.

Potency itself is personified by Sir David Lyndsay (1486–1555) in the character of Sensualitie, from his serio-comic morality play *Ane Pleasant Satyre of the Thrie Estaitis*, the last performance of which in the author's lifetime took place in Edinburgh only six years before the Reformation. Although Lyndsay never formally renounced his allegiance to Catholicism, after his death he was discovered to have possessed a copy of the Bible in English, at that period an heretical offence, and in his play the forces of disorder, including the seductive Sensualitie, are eventually defeated by the spirit of reform. Yet Lyndsay's own enjoyment of bawdry is unmistakably proclaimed in his hilarious scenes of knockabout sexual farce, and he may be counted fortunate to have given up the ghost before the Calvinists imposed their puritanical creed on kirk and country. Not that the Calvinists ever entirely succeeded in scotching the old Adam whom they sought so zealously to suppress. The first Alexander Scott, who lived through the immediate Reformation years, was sufficiently sympathetic to Protestant aims to provide Scots versions of some psalms, yet he remains unrivalled except by Burns as a composer of love-songs, and his 'Up, Helsum Hairt' bids fair to be the most evocative and not the least explicit aubade in the language. Throughout the seventeenth century, too, the Cavaliers—members of the Court-party—maintained their resistance to Calvinist extremism, William Drummond of Hawthornden (1585–1649) and Francis Semple of Beltrees (*c.* 1616–1682) expressing, either in the "golden" Renaissance style or in the folksong mode, those actualities of naked fact and feeling whose fire defies the freezing dictates of theological dogma.

In the eighteenth century, resistance to Calvinist rigour becomes explicit and overt, emboldened no doubt by the influence of more liberal attitudes from south of the Border—for Scottish poetry from now on is in fact Anglo-Scottish poetry, even those writers from the middle and labouring classes whose native tongue is Scots composing sometimes in that medium and sometimes in English, and all of them shaped to some extent, either greater or lesser, by the literature of England as well as by a native folk-tradition that had escaped the oblivion into which the art-poetry of the great medieval Scots makars had fallen after the Union of the Crowns and the adoption of English as the language of educated discourse in Scotland. In part, the anti-Calvinist reaction takes the form of satire of puritan sexual hypocrisy, as in Ramsay's 'The Marrow Ballad' and Burns's 'Holy Willie's Prayer', while the obverse of the same coin stands out blatantly in the four-letter words propagated by the anonymous bawdy folksongs and those songs by Burns which represent the culminating climax of the same avowedly immodest mode.

Yet, at the same time, the uneasy awareness of the depravity of illicit sex and the puritanical identification of passion with original sin, as notable in the first Alexander Scott's satires on wanton women and blinded lovers as is his glorification of sexual love in 'Up, Helsum Hairt', have persisted to the present century, whether they are scoffed at, as in passages of Hugh MacDiarmid's *A Drunk Man Looks at the Thistle* (1926), or derisively dismissed, as in Tom Leonard's 'Pffff' (1975). (The fact that Mr Leonard is not a Calvinist by birth and education but a Scotch-Irish Catholic is immaterial, since Scotch-Irish Catholicism today is far closer to the old-fashioned puritanism of Reform than that movement's "degenerate" descendants in the contemporary Kirk of Scotland.) The ironical contrast between sex and sanctity in Maurice Lindsay's 'Dans La Piscine', the satirical sketch of Burns on heat in hellfire in the present writer's 'Burns Burns', the wry attempted escape from sexual guilt in Alastair Mackie's 'Adam and Eve', the conscious comic defiance of biblical prohibition of desire in W. Price Turner's 'Driven at Night', and the burlesque assault on the Lenin of our Reformation in Alan Jackson's 'Knox', are all evidence of the same syndrome.

Yet another religion, far older than Calvin and even more ancient than Catholicism, has persisted too—the witchcraft of the greatest of the traditional Scottish ballads of the supernatural, endeared to poets who have enjoyed the fecund sexuality of the witch as the polar opposite of the conventional worship of the pallid virgin. In the ballad of 'Tam Lin' the mettlesome young heroine is already pregnant by the markedly masculine witch-boy when she rescues him from the Queen of Elfland; in Burns's 'Tam o' Shanter' the one youthful witch whose near-nakedness electrifies the hero is magnetically desirable; in 'May of the Moril Glen' by James Hogg (1770–1836) the compelling charms of that wonderwoman are quite literally fatal to the wives of all her willing victims; in 'The Witch's Ballad' by William Bell Scott (1811–1890) the heroine and her friends dazzle a whole township with their beauty and lead the townsmen a daring dance; in MacDiarmid's 'Bride' the mystic newlywed is forever ravished and forever magically remade a maiden; in 'The Tryst' by William Soutar (1898–1943) the glamorous creature who comes to the poet's bed in the night vanishes away before dawn like a supernatural visitant. Glamour—in its Scottish sense of witchcraft—is attributed to all young women in the editor's 'Love is a Garth', and in his 'Monstrous!' the irresistible witches of legend become contemporary as the enchanting anti-heroines of horror films.

Paganism also lives on, partly as a reaction against the aberrant Christianity of puritanism, partly in order to glorify Eros through deification. Both aspects are evident in the extracts given here from Burns's 'The Vision' and from 'A Ballad in Blank Verse of the Making of a Poet' by John Davidson (1857–1909). On the other hand, Drummond of Hawthornden's portrait of the girl as goddess is all glorification, as is the picture of 'The Young Audh' in MacDiarmid's Anglo-Scottish version of Rilke. Yet even when Eros is deified, elements of the old Scottish distrust of the destructive power of passion may still remain, as in the savage repudiation of sexual desire in 'Cupid and Venus' by Mark Alexander Boyd (1563–1601) or in the brutal reduction of god and goddess to "a drucken jock wi a drucken hure" in Goodsir Smith's 'Mars and Venus at Hogmanay'. Or the poet may be ambivalent in his attitudes, like Norman MacCaig (b. 1910), whose 'Classical Translation' and 'Goddess of Lust' are equally elegant although the first expresses acceptance of every element of passion while the second rejects its diminishment into desire divorced from love.

Not only pagan legend, however, but also the more mythological aspects of the Christian story, have provided opportunities for deifying Eros for those Scottish poets to whom nothing (or all) is sacred in the attempt to express the inexpressible reality of physical rapture. Edwin Muir (1887–1959) in 'The Annunciation' and Hugh MacDiarmid in 'Harry Semen' have produced two of the most astonishing achievements in the whole canon of Scottish poetry. The encounter between angel and mortal maiden in the former and the sanctification of human seed in the latter are inexplicable in terms of prose comment, and these truly miraculous poems must be left to speak (or sing) for themselves.

The many other Scottish poems of Eros exultant and/or enraptured are concerned with more mundane—if scarcely less marvellous—delights, and the line runs unbroken throughout the whole tradition, from King James' first entranced awareness of his lady in the early fifteenth century to the explosive contact with his girl experienced by the youngest poet in the anthology, Andrew Greig (b. 1951), writing in the last quarter of the twentieth. The variations which it is possible to play upon those themes appear to be inexhaustible, and they are also as irresistible as the passion they exist to celebrate. Here the shadows of doubt and distrust which gloom around the erotic in other verses are burned away by the all-consuming blaze of joy. This is a poetry of affirmation, as frank as it is free.

Almost all of Scottish erotic verse is happily heterosexual, and most of the handful of poems on sexual aberrations are either burlesques, like Dunbar's 'This Hindir Nicht' and Burns's 'A Bonie Hen', both of which derive from the beast-fable tradition, or witty satires in the mode of assumed broadmindedness, like Alexander Robertson's 'Ode' and William J. Tait's 'Ane o Nature's'. The two exceptions here are both contemporary, and both—in their individual

ways—tragic. 'Sappho' by Robin Hamilton (b. 1945) expresses a desperate
lesbian attempt at self-justification, while Edwin Morgan's 'Christmas Eve', on
a homosexual encounter (or rather, failure to encounter), reveals a horrified
and horrifying denial of an utterly barren desire. The extension of range
represented by these remarkable works reveals the continuing capacity of the
tradition to explore and occupy new ground.

The editor of this selection has taken its title—with perhaps characteristic
immodesty—from a two-word epigram of his own:

SCOTCH PASSION
Forgot
Mysel.

It may be that this jest encapsulates the fundamental distinction between the
erotic poetry anthologised here and the pornographic verse which nowadays
pullulates from the Press. In the first as in the last analysis, pornographic verse
resembles the pin-up photograph, which is its pictorial equivalent, in being
masturbation material. But Eros reaches out to embrace The Other.

1

Eros Deified

SENSUALITY*

Luifers awalk! behald the fyrie spheir,
Behauld the naturall dochter of Venus:
Behauld luifers, this lustie ladie cleir,
The fresche fonteine of knichtis amorous,
Repleit with joyis dulce and delicious.
Or quha wald mak to Venus observance,
In my mirthfull chalmer melodious,
There sall thay fynd all pastyme, and pleasance;

Behauld my heid, behauld my gay attyre,
Behauld my halse, lusum and lilie quhyte;
Behauld my visage, flammand as the fyre,
Behauld my papis, of portratour perfyte.
To luik on mee luiffers hes greit delyte,
Rycht sa hes all the kinges of Christindome;
To thame I haif done pleasouris infinyte,
And speciallie unto the Court of Rome.

Ane kis of me war worth, in ane morning,
A milyioun of gold to knight, or king:
And yit, I am of nature sa towart,
I lat na luiffer pas with ane sair hart.
Of my name, wald ye wit the veritie,
Forsuith thay call me Sensualitie.
I hauld it best now, or we farther gang,
To dame Venus let us go sing ane Sang.

Sir David Lyndsay (1486–1555)

CUPID AND VENUS*

Fra banc to banc, fra wod to wod, I rin
Ourhailit with my feble fantasie,
Lyc til a leif that fallis from a trie
Or til a reid ourblawin with the wind.
Twa gods gyds me: the ane of tham is blind,
Ye, and a bairn brocht up in vanitie;
The nixt a wyf ingenrit of the se,
And lichter nor a dauphin with hir fin.

Unhappie is the man for evirmaire
That teils the sand and sawis in the aire;
Bot twyse unhappier is he, I lairn,
That feidis in his hairt a mad desyre,
And follows on a woman throw the fyre,
Led be a blind and teichit be a bairn.

Mark Alexander Boyd (1563–1601)

GIRL GODDESS*

Like the Idalian Queene
Her haire about her eyne,
With neck and brests ripe apples to be seene,
At first glance of the morn
In Cyprus gardens gathering those faire flowers
Which of her bloud were borne,
I saw, but fainting saw, my paramours.
The Graces naked danc'd about the place,
The winds and trees amaz'd
With silence on her gaz'd,
The flowrs did smile, like those upon her face,
And as their aspine stalkes those fingers band,
(That shee might read my case)
A hyacinth I wisht mee in her hand.

William Drummond (1585–1649)

LEG-MAN*

When click! the string the snick did draw;
And jee! the door gaed to the wa';
And by my ingle-lowe I saw,

Now bleezan bright,
A tight, outlandish hizzie, braw,
Come full in sight.

Green, slender, leaf-clad holly-boughs
Were twisted, gracefu', round her brows,
I took her for some SCOTTISH MUSE,
By that same token;
And come to stop those reckless vows,
Would soon be broken.

A 'hare-brain'd, sentimental trace'
Was strongly marked in her face;
A wildly-witty, rustic grace
Shone full upon her;
Her eye, ev'n turn'd on empty space,
Beam'd keen with honour.

Down flow'd her robe, a tartan sheen,
Till half a leg was scrimply seen;
And such a leg! my bonie JEAN
Could only peer it;
Sae straught, sae taper, tight and clean,
Nane else came near it.

Robert Burns (1759–1796)

THE ADVENT OF APHRODITE*

He beheld
The Cyprian Aphrodite, all one blush
And glance of passion, from the violet sea
Step inland, fastening as she went her zone.
She reached a gulf that opened in the ground
Deep in a leafless wood and waited there,
Battling the darkness with her wistful eyes.
Then suddenly she blanched and blushed again,
And her divinely pulsing body bowed
With outstretched arms over the yawning earth.
Straightway Adonis, wonderstruck and pale,
Stole from the sepulchre, a moonbeam wraith.
But Aphrodite with a golden cry
That echoed round the world and shook the stars,

Caught him and thawed him in her warm embrace,
And murmuring kisses bore him to her bower.
Then all the trees were lit with budding flames
Of emerald, and all the meads and leas,
Coverts and shady places, glades and dells,
Odoured and dimly stained with opening flowers,
And loud with love-songs of impassioned birds,
Became the shrine and hostel of the spring.

His wanton face grew sweet and wonderful,
Beholding Aphrodite . . .
                                    "Oh, let me be!"
The dreamer cried, and rushing from the house
He sought the outcast Aphrodite, dull,
Tawdry, unbeautiful, but still divine
Even in the dark streets of a noisome port.

But in the evening by the purple firth
He walked, and saw brown locks upon the brine
And pale hands beckon him to come away.

John Davidson (1857–1909)

THE ANNUNCIATION

The angel and the girl are met.
Earth was the only meeting place.
For the embodied never yet
Travelled beyond the shore of space.
The eternal spirits in freedom go.

See, they have come together, see,
While the destroying minutes flow,
Each reflects the other's face
Till heaven in hers and earth in his
Shine steady there. He's come to her
From far beyond the farthest star,
Feathered through time. Immediacy
Of strangest strangeness is the bliss
That from their limbs all movement takes.
Yet the increasing rapture brings
So great a wonder that it makes
Each feather tremble on his wings.

Outside the window footsteps fall
Into the ordinary day
And with the sun along the wall
Pursue their unreturning way.
Sound's perpetual roundabout
Rolls its numbered octaves out
And hoarsely grinds its battered tune.

But through the endless afternoon
These neither speak nor movement make,
But stare into their deepening trance
As if their gaze would never break.

Edwin Muir (1887–1959)

HARRY SEMEN*

I ken these islands each inhabited
Forever by a single man
Livin' in his separate world as only
In dreams yet maist folk can.

Mine's like the moonwhite belly o' a hoo
Seen in the water as a fisher draws in his line.
I canna land it nor can it ever brak awa'.
It never moves, yet seems a' movement in the brine;
A movin' picture o' the spasm frae which I was born,
It writhes again, and back to it I'm willy-nilly torn.
A' men are similarly fixt; and the difference 'twixt
    The sae-ca'd sane and insane
Is that the latter whiles ha'e glimpses o't
    And the former nane.

Particle frae particle'll brak asunder,
Ilk ane o' them mair livid than the neist.
A separate life?—incredible war o' equal lichts,
Nane o' them wi' ocht in common in the least.
Nae threid o' a' the fabric o' my thocht
Is left alangside anither; a pack
O' leprous scuts o' weasels riddlin' a plaid
    Sic thrums could never mak'.
Hoo mony shades o' white gaed curvin' owre
To yon blae centre o' her belly's flower?

Milk-white, and dove-grey, wi' harebell veins.
Ae scar in fair hair like the sun in sunlicht lay,
And pelvic experience in a thin shadow line;
Thocht canna mairry thocht as sic saft shadows dae.

Grey ghastly commentaries on my puir life,
A' the sperm that's gane for naething rises up to damn
In sick-white onanism the single seed
Frae which in sheer irrelevance I cam.
What were the odds against me? Let me coont.
What worth am I to a' that micht ha'e been?
To a' the wasted slime I'm capable o'
Appeals this lurid emission, whirlin' lint-white and green.
Am I alane richt, solidified to life,
Disjoined frae a' this searin' like a white-het knife,
And vauntin' my alien accretions here,
Boastin' sanctions, purpose, sense the endless tide
I cam frae lacks—the tide I still sae often feed?
O bitter glitter; wet sheet and flowin' sea—and what beside?

Sae the bealin' continents lie upon the seas,
     Sprawlin' in shapeless shápes o' airts,
Like ony splash that ony man can mak'
     Frae his nose or throat or ither pairts,
Fantastic as ink through blottin'-paper rins.
But this is white, white like a flooerin' gean,
Passin' frae white to purer shades o' white,
Ivory, crystal, diamond, till nae difference is seen
Between its fairest blossoms and the stars.
Or the clear sun they melt into,
And the wind mixes them amang each ither
Forever, hue upon still mair dazzlin' hue.

Sae Joseph may ha'e pondered; sae a snawstorm
Comes whirlin' in grey sheets frae the shadowy sky
And only in a sma' circle are the separate flakes seen.
White, whiter, they cross and recross as capricious they fly,
Mak' patterns on the grund and weave into wreaths,
Load the bare boughs, and find lodgements in corners frae
The scourin' wind that sends a snawstorm up frae the earth
To meet that frae the sky, till which is which nae man can say.

They melt in the waters. They fill the valleys. They scale the peaks.
There's a tinkle o' icicles. The topmaist summit shines oot.
Sae Joseph may ha'e pondered on the coiled fire in his seed,
The transformation in Mary, and seen Jesus tak' root.

Hugh MacDiarmid (1892–1978)

THE YOUNG AUDH*
(*From the German of Rainer Maria Rilke*)

Upon that morning following the night
Which anxiously had passed with calls, unrest
And tumult, all the sea broke up once more
And cried. And when the crying slowly closed
Again and from the pallid day and heaven's
Beginning fell within the chasm of mute fish:
The sea brought forth.

And with the earliest sun the hairfoam
Of the waves' broad vulva shimmered, on whose rim
The girl stood upright, white, confused, and wet.
Just as a young green leaf bestirs itself
And stretches forth and slow unfurls its inrolled
Whorlings, so her body's form unfolded into coolness,
And into the untouched early wind.
As moons the knees rose upwards clear and dived
Within the cloudy outlines of the thighs.
The narrow shadow of the legs retreated
And the feet grew tightened and became as light
As silence and the joints lived like the throats
Of drinking ones.

And in the hollow of the hip's deep bowl
The belly lay and seemed a fresh young fruit
Within a child's hand. In its navel's narrow
Cup was all the darkness of this brilliant life.
A little wave below it lightly raised
Itself and ever sped across towards the loins,
Whereon from time to time a silent rippling was.
But all translumined and already without shadow,
Like a copse of silver birches pale in April,
Warm and empty and unhidden lay the sex.

Now stood the shoulders' poised and mobile scales
In perfect balance on the upright body,
Which from the bowl of hips arose as though
It were a fountain, downward falling,
Hesitating in the long and slender arms,
And faster in the fullest fall of hair.

Then went the face quite slowly past;
From out the deep foreshortened darkness of
Its inclination into clear and horizontal
High-upliftedness. And 'neath it was the chin closed steeply
And when the throat was now forthstretched and seemed
A water-ray of flowerstem in which sap rose,
The arms stretched also forth like necks of swans
Who seek the shore.

Then came into this body's darkened earliness
Like morning wind the first indrawal of breath.
Within the tender branching of the veintrees
There arose a whispering and the blood began
To purl and murmur o'er its deepest places.
And this wind increased: it threw itself
With every breath into the newborn breasts
And filled them full and pressed far into them—
So that like sails, full of the distances,
They urged the windlight maiden t'wards the shore.

So landed the goddess.

Behind her,
Quickly stepping through the young green shores,
The flowers and flower-stalks raised themselves
All morning long, confused and warm, as though
From deep embraces. And she went, and ran.

But at the noon of day, all in the heaviest hour,
The ocean once more roused itself and threw
Upon the self-same spot a dolphin.
Dead, red and open.

Hugh MacDiarmid (1892–1978)

GODDESS OF LUST

Her coif, her coiffure,
Her watch-chain ankles
Make dizzy the air
In igloos and Insurance Offices.
Airports remember her,
Cafés wear her scent.

She saunters with mirrors
Through holy congregations—
She's everywhere: except
She has always just left
The million sad rooms
Where love lies weeping.

Norman MacCaig (b. 1910)

CLASSICAL TRANSLATION

Venus, familiar name, means
thinking of you.

I love Venus and she smiles on me
with no condescension.

She comes to me like eyes, like hair,
like breasts. She comes like laughter
and sad weeping.

The other gods move off—spluttering Mars,
manic Naptune, even Pluto—even,
to my grief, friendly Apollo.

But wise Minerva stays near.
She whispers to me the meaning
of eyes and hair and breasts. She tells me
how your laughter and your weeping
are the children of Venus
and are not to be separated.

Norman MacCaig (b. 1910)

MARS AND VENUS AT HOGMANAY*

The nicht is deep,
The snaw liggs crisp wi rime,
Black and cauld the leafless trees;
Midnicht, but nae bells chime.

Throu the tuim white sleepan street
Mars and Venus shauchle past,
A drucken jock wi a drucken hure
Rairan 'The Ball o Kirriemuir'!

Sydney Goodsir Smith (1915–1975)

＊

2

Eros Calvinized

THE MARROW BALLAD*

O fy, let us a' to the meeting,
   For there will be canting there,
Where some will be laughing, some greeting,
   At the preaching of Erskine and Mair.
Then rouze ye up, Robie and Willy!
   The lassies are raiking awa,
In petty-coats white as the lilly,
   And biggonets prind on fou braw.

And there will be blinkan eyed Bessy,
   Blyth Baby, and sweet lipet Megg,
And mony a rosie cheek'd lassie
   With coats kiltet to their mid-legg.
To gar them gang clever and lightly,
   We'll carry their hose and their shoon;
Syne kiss them and clap them fou tightly,
   As soon as the sermon is done.

The sun will be sunk in the west
   Before they have finished the wark:
Then behind a whin bush we can rest,
   There's meikle good done in the dark.
There Tammy to Tibby may creep,
   Slee Sandy may mool in with Kate;
While other dowf sauls are asleep,
   We'll handle deep matters of state.

And shou'd we deserve the black stools,
   For geting a gamphrell with wean,
We'll answer we're no siccan fools
   To obey them that have the oaths tane.

When the lave's to the parish kirk gawn,
  On Sundays—we'll rest us at hame,
An' running to hills now and than
  Maks it nowther a sin nor a shame.

Then up with the brethren true blew,
  Wha leads us to siccan delight,
And can prove it, altho they be few,
  That there is naebody else wha is right.
And doun with all government laws,
  That are made by the Bishops of Baal,
And the thieves wha climb o'er the kirk waws
  And come not in by a right call.

Allan Ramsay (1686–1758)

GODLY GIRZY*

The night it was a haly night,
  The day had been a haly day;
Kilmarnock gleam'd wi' candle light
  As Girzie hameward took her way.
A man o' sin, ill may he thrive!
  And never haly-meeting see!
Wi' godly Girzie met belyve,
  Amang the Cragie hills sae hie.

The chiel' was wight, the chiel' was stark,
  He wad na wait to chap nor ca',
And she was faint wi' haly wark,
  She had na pith to say him na.
But ay she glowr'd up to the moon,
  And ay she sigh'd most piouslie;
"I trust my heart 's in heaven aboon,
  "Whare'er your sinfu' pintle be."

Robert Burns (1759–1796)

A TALE OF A WIFE*

I'll tell you a tale of a wife,
  And she was a Whig and a saunt;
She liv'd a most sanctify'd life,
  But whyles she was fash'd wi' her cunt.

Poor woman!—she gaed to the priest,
　　And till him she made her complaint;
"There's naething that troubles my breast
　　"Sae sair as the sins o' my cunt.

"Sin that I was herdin at hame,
　　"Till now I'm three score and ayont,
"I own it wi' sin and wi' shame
　　"I've led a sad life wi' my cunt."

He bade her to clear up her brow,
　　And no be discourag'd upon 't;
For holy gude women enow
　　Were mony times waur't wi' their cunt.

It's naught but Beelzebub's art,
　　But that's the mair sign of a saunt,
He kens that ye're pure at the heart,
　　Sae levels his darts at your cunt.

What signifies morals and works,
　　Our works are no wordy a runt!
It's faith that is sound, orthodox,
　　That covers the fauts o' your cunt.

Were ye o' the reprobate race
　　Created to sin and be brunt,
O then it would alter the case
　　If ye should gae wrang wi' your cunt.

But you that is called and free
　　Elekit and chosen a saunt,
Will 't break the Eternal Decree
　　Whatever ye do wi' your cunt?

And now with a sanctify'd kiss
　　Let's kneel and renew covenant:
It's this—and it's this—and it's this—
　　That settles the pride o' your cunt.

Devotion blew up to a flame;
　　No words can do justice upon 't;
The honest auld woman gaed hame
　　Rejoicin and clawin her cunt.

Then high to her memory charge;
  And may he who takes it affront,
Still ride in Love's channel at large,
  And never make port in a cunt!!!

Robert Burns (1759–1796)

HOLY WILLIE*

But yet—O Lord—confess I must—
At times I'm fash'd wi' fleshly lust;
And sometimes too, in warldly trust
   Vile self gets in;
But thou remembers we are dust,
   Defil'd wi' sin.

O Lord—yestreen—thou kens—wi' Meg—
   Thy pardon I sincerely beg!
O may 't ne'er be a living plague
   To my dishonour!
And I'll ne'er lift a lawless leg
   Again upon her.

Besides, I farther maun avow,
Wi' Leezie's lass, three times—I trow—
But Lord, that Friday I was fou
   When I cam near her;
Or else, thou kens, thy servant true
   Wad never steer her.

Maybe thou lets this fleshy thorn
Buffet thy servant e'en and morn,
Lest he o'er proud and high should turn,
   That he's sae gifted;
If sae, thy hand maun e'en be borne
   Untill thou lift it.

Robert Burns (1759–1796)

THE ANNUNCIATION*

The tug-o'-war is in me still,
The dog-hank o' the flesh and soul—
Faither in Heaven, what gar'd ye tak'

A village slut to mither me,
Your mongrel o' the fire and clay?
The trollop and the Deity share
My writhen form as tho' I were
A picture o' the time they had
When Licht rejoiced to file itsel'
And Earth upshuddered like a star.

A drucken hizzie gane to bed
Wi' three-in-ane and ane-in-three.

Hugh MacDiarmid (1892–1978)

THE THISTLE IN THE WIND

The thistle in the wind dissolves
In lichtnin's as shook foil gie's way
In sudden splendours, or the flesh
As Daith lets slip the infinite soul;
And syne it's like a sunrise tint
In grey o' day, or love and life
That in a cloody blash o' sperm
Undae the warld to big't again,
Or like a pickled foetus that
Nae man feels ocht in common wi'
—But micht as easily ha' been!
Or like a corpse a soul set free
Scunners to think it tenanted
—And little recks that but for it
It never micht ha' been at a',
Like love frae lust and God frae man!

The wasted seam that dries like stairch
And pooders aff, that micht ha' been
A warld o' men and syne o' Gods;
The grey that haunts the vievest green;
The wrang side o' the noblest scene
We ne'er can whummle to oor een,
As 'twere the hinderpairts o' God,
His face aye turned the opposite road,
Or's neth the floo'ers the drumlie clods
Frae which they come at sicna odds,
As a' Earth's magic frae a spirt,
In shame and secrecy, o' dirt!

Hugh MacDiarmid (1892–1978)

I WISH I KENT

I wish I kent the physical basis
O' a' life's seemin' airs and graces.

It's queer the thochts a kittled cull
Can lowse or splairgin' glit annul.

Man's spreit is wi' his ingangs twined
In ways that he can ne'er unwind.

A wumman whiles a bawaw gi'es
That clean abaws him gin he sees.

Or wi' a movement o' a leg
Shows'm his mind is juist a geg.

I'se warrant Jean 'ud no' be lang
In findin' whence this thistle sprang!

Mebbe it's juist because I'm no'
Beddit wi' her that gars it grow!

Hugh MacDiarmid (1892–1978)

DANS LA PISCINE

However much our expectations hone us,
we can't predict when life declares a bonus:
these *Glorias* described by holy men,
nothings that tremble on their edge, and then
sink back into their rounded drone of praise
the rest of us think ordinary days.

A brief bikini by an open pool,
teaching a splash of youngsters swimming's rule,
her hair, her neck, her settled mien, her face
what sinful men conceive the look of grace;
the lift of her breasts, her belly's gentle curve,
a skin that rippled litheness with each move,
she stooped to her concerns, and seemed to be
the ripe perfection of virginity.

Swimming decades apart, I warmed to watch
her bend away and shape a cotton crotch
where some man's hand would kindle a new fire,
heating her to his own and time's desire.
Yet for a fitting moment, there she stands,
unplucked, with others' children on her hands,
as if unconscious of the flesh's need
for love to pull her down, and swell and breed.

How many *Hallelujahs* would you raise,
you holy men, for one such worshipped gaze!
I've had a cold shower in the best tradition
to keep my doubtful soul from your perdition,
and strop the towel of penance on your lack
of absolution, mopping up my back.

Maurice Lindsay (b. 1918)

BURNS BURNS

Whan Burns was deid and damned to hell
   For rhymes and houghmagandies,
   He socht the hinney randies
He'd pleased in pleasan maist himsel.

He socht them doun i the doolie deeps
   Whaur fiercest fire was lowean,
   The pyne for merry mowein
That canty limmers thole for keeps.

But fient the kissan phizz he fand
   (And fient the wame or hurdies)
   O' aa the bonnie burdies
He'd served wi mair nor hert and hand.

"Hou cam I here in hell my lane?"
   He speired at hotteran Hornie;
   The Thief's repone was thorny:
"The faut, ye fule, is aa your ain!

"Your sangs wad saunt the lichtliest quine
   That lay in your airms unsarkit,
   Till even THE MAKAR markit
The wey your sinners seemed divine.

''For love, could GOD THE LORD dae less
　　Nor you wi your mortal scrievin?
　　He's heisted your jos to Heaven,
The angels' unco-guid address.

''But you, wi your daft 'Address to the Deil,'
　　He's damned to the bleeze for blockin,
　　And never a lass to slocken
The lowe o the hellfire love ye feel.''

Alexander Scott (b. 1920)

ADAM AND EVE

In the black dark o the bed-room
the muckle ee o God—
Him that sees aathing—
looks doun
on twa bodies
His thooms drappit
rib neist rib.

Aipple ye are
and lang teen trail o a worm,
Eve-deil.
I straik your fruit
skin whaur the serpent skouks.
I tak the first bite.
Adam, dammt.

I'm smittit
wi the pest in ye.
I grou worm
and aipple baith.

He watches twa worms
fechtin.

Good or ill
we ken neither.
Like beasts
beasts o the field.

Wi the sweat o oor broo
we earn peace,
oor nicht-darg ower.

Swaalowin ane anither
in oor book
is naebody's wyte.

Alastair Mackie (b. 1925)

DRIVEN AT NIGHT

With another man's wife I share space
in the back of another man's car.
This is the only life I've got
and here I am staking it
on another's skill and care.
There's no shaking it,
he drives well. Beside me, she seems
to sleep as lights caress her face.
If this is lust, I'm slaking it
by courtesy of her dreams.
But I know my place:
there's no mistaking it,
even when that fat pimp, the moon,
contrives to dwell on her flesh, making it
seem unreal by some remote amendment.
We'll be free, separately, soon,
of this shut-in moving mesh
that has me taking it
seriously. Here is the tenth commandment,
and this is Bill Turner breaking it.

W. Price Turner (b. 1927)

KNOX

in the pub
          where the hundred fastest women in Glasgow go
to get Americans
     I put my hand on my girlfriend's breast.
Quick as a flash the barman comes up and says:
     "Cut that out, son. This is a public bar."

Scotch Passion

O Knox he was a bad man
he split the Scottish mind.
The one half he made cruel
and the other half unkind.
As for you, as for you, as for you, auld Jesus lad,
gawn dance the nails fae oot yer taes, an
try an be mair glad.

Alan Jackson (b. 1938)

PFFFF*

guhta light

                    fuck me
                    skirt upty here
                    thaht size

tah

                    jeezus crise tam
                    wee firm arss yi no
                    whuht kinyi day

pffff

                    middla Sucky Hall Street
                    fuckin big hard dawn
                    nearly shot ma load

pffff

                    its no right thaht naw
                    naw its no right thaht

pffff

                    bluddy blaizir oanur tay
                    stullit fuckin skool

Tom Leonard (b. 1944)

3

Eros Bewitching

TAM LIN*

O I forbid you, maidens a'
   That wear gowd on your hair,
To come, or gae by Carterhaugh,
   For young Tom-lin is there.

There 's nane that gaes by Carterhaugh
   But they leave him a wad;
Either their rings, or green mantles,
   Or else their maidenhead.

Janet has kilted her green kirtle,
   A little aboon her knee;
And she has broded her yellow hair
   A little aboon her bree;
And she 's awa to Carterhaugh
   As fast as she can hie.

When she cam to Carterhaugh
   Tom-lin was at the well,
And there she fand his steed standing
   But away was himsel.

She had na pu'd a double rose,
   A rose but only tway,
Till up then started young Tom-lin,
   Says, Lady, thou 's pu' nae mae.

Why pu's thou the rose, Janet,
   And why breaks thou the wand?
Or why comes thou to Carterhaugh
   Withoutten my command?

Carterhaugh it is my ain,
  Ma daddie gave it me;
I'll come and gang by Carterhaugh
  And ask nae leave at thee.

Janet has kilted her green kirtle
  A little aboon her knee,
And she has snooded her yellow hair,
  A little aboon her bree,
And she is to her father's ha,
  As fast as she can hie.

Four and twenty ladies fair
  Were playing at the ba,
And out then cam the fair Janet,
  Ance the flower amang them 'a.

Four and twenty ladies fair
  Were playing at the chess,
And out then cam the fair Janet,
  As green as onie glass.

Out then spak an auld grey knight,
  Lay o'er the castle-wa,
And says, Alas, fair Janet for thee
  But we'll be blamed a'.

Haud your tongue ye auld-fac'd knight,
  Some ill death may ye die,
Father my bairn on whom I will,
  I'll father nane on thee.

Out then spak her father dear,
  And he spak meek and mild,
And ever alas, sweet Janet, he says,
  I think thou gaes wi' child.

If that I gae wi' child, father,
  Mysel maun bear the blame;
There 's ne'er a laird about your ha,
  Shall get the bairn's name.

If my Love were an earthly knight,
  As he 's an elfin grey;

I wad na gie my ain true-love
   For nae lord that ye hae.

The steed that my true-love rides on
   Is lighter than the wind;
Wi' siller he is shod before,
   Wi' burning gowd behind.

Janet has kilted her green kirtle
   A little aboon her knee;
And she has snooded her yellow hair
   A little aboon her brie;
And she 's awa to Carterhaugh
   As fast as she can hie.

When she cam to Carterhaugh,
   Tom-lin was at the well;
And there she fand his steed standing,
   But away was himsel.

She had na pu'd a double rose,
   A rose but only tway,
Till up then started young Tom-lin,
   Says, Lady thou pu's nae mae.

Why pu's thou the rose, Janet,
   Amang the groves sae green,
And a' to kill the bonie babe
   That we gat us between.

O tell me, tell me, Tom-lin she says,
   For 's sake that died on tree,
If e'er ye was in holy chapel,
   Or Christendom did see.

Roxburgh he was my grandfather,
   Took me with him to bide,
And ance it fell upon a day
   That wae did me betide.

Ance it fell upon a day,
   A cauld day and a snell,
When we were frae the hunting come
   That frae my horse I fell.

The queen o' Fairies she caught me,
   In yon green hill to dwell,
And pleasant is the fairy-land;
   But, an eerie tale to tell!

Ay at the end of seven years
   We pay a tiend to hell;
I am sae fair and fu' of flesh
   I'm fear'd it be mysel.

But the night is Halloween, lady,
   The morn is Hallowday;
Then win me, win me, an ye will,
   For weel I wat ye may.

Just at the mirk and midnight hour
   The fairy folk will ride;
And they that wad their truelove win,
   At Milescross they maun bide.

But how shall I thee ken, Tom-lin,
   O how my truelove know,
Amang sae mony unco knights
   The like I never saw.

O first let pass the black, Lady,
   And syne let pass the brown;
But quickly run to the milk-white steed,
   Pu ye his rider down:

For I'll ride on the milk-white steed,
   And ay nearest the town;
Because I was an earthly knight
   They gie me that renown.

My right hand will be glov'd, lady,
   My left hand will be bare;
Cockt up shall my bonnet be,
   And kaim'd down shall my hair;
And thae 's the tokens I gie thee,
   Nae doubt I will be there.

They'll turn me in your arms, lady,
   Into an ask and adder,

But hald me fast and fear me not,
   I am your bairn's father.

They'll turn me to a bear sae grim,
   And then a lion bold;
But hold me fast and fear me not,
   As ye shall love your child.

Again they'll turn me in your arms
   To a red het gaud of airn;
But hold me fast and fear me not,
   I'll do to you nae harm.

And last they'll turn me, in your arms,
   Into the burning lead;
Then throw me into well-water,
   O throw me in wi' speed!

And then I'll be your ain truelove,
   I'll turn a naked knight:
Then cover me wi' your green mantle,
   And cover me out o sight.

Gloomy, gloomy was the night,
   And eerie was the way,
As fair Jenny in her green mantle
   To Milescross she did gae.

About the middle o' the night
   She heard the bridles ring;
This lady was as glad at that
   As any earthly thing.

First she let the black pass by,
   And syne she let the brown;
But quickly she ran to the milk-white steed,
   And pu'd the rider down.

Sae weel she minded what he did say
   And young Tom-lin did win;
Syne cover'd him wi' her green mantle
   As blythe 's a bird in spring.

Out then spak the queen o' Fairies,
   Out of a bush o' broom;
Them that has gotten young Tom-lin,
   Has gotten a stately groom.

Out then spak the queen o' Fairies,
   And an angry queen was she;
Shame betide her ill-fard face,
   And an ill death may she die,
For she 's ta'en awa the boniest knight
   In a' my companie.

But had I kend, Tom-lin, she says,
   What now this night I see,
I wad hae taen out thy twa grey een,
   And put in twa een o' tree.

Traditional, communicated by Robert Burns

CUTTY SARK*

As Tammie glow'rd, amaz'd, and curious,
The mirth and fun grew fast and furious:
The piper loud and louder blew;
The dancers quick and quicker flew;
They reel'd, they set, they cross'd, they cleekit,
Till ilka carlin swat and reekit,
And coost her duddies to the wark,
And linket at it in her sark!

Now, Tam, O Tam! had thae been queans,
A' plump and strapping in their teens,
Their sarks, instead o' creeshie flannen,
Been snaw-white seventeen hunder linnen!
Thir breeks o' mine, my only pair,
That ance were plush, o' gude blue hair,
I wad hae gi'en them off my hurdies,
For ae blink o' the bonie burdies!

But wither'd beldams, auld and droll,
Rigwoodie hags wad spean a foal,
Lowping and flinging on a crummock,
I wonder didna turn thy stomach.

But Tam kent what was what fu' brawlie,
There was ae winsome wench and wawlie,
That night enlisted in the core,
(Lang after kend on Carrick shore;
For mony a beast to dead she shot,
And perished mony a bony boat,
And shook baith meikle corn and bear,
And kept the country-side in fear:)
Her cutty sark, o' Paisley harn,
That while a lassie she had worn,
In longitude tho' sorely scanty,
It was her best, and she was vauntie.—
Ah! little kend thy reverend grannie,
That sark she coft for her wee Nannie,
Wi' twa pund Scots, ('twas a' her riches),
Wad ever grac'd a dance of witches!

But here my Muse her wing maun cour;
Sic flights are far beyond her pow'r;
To sing how Nannie lap and flang,
(A souple jade she was, and strang),
And how Tam stood, like ane bewitched,
And thought his very een enrich'd;
Even Satan glowr'd, and fidg'd fu' fain,
And hotch'd and blew wi' might and main:
Till first ae caper, syne anither,
Tam tint his reason a' thegither,
And roars out, "Weel done, Cutty-sark!"
And in an instant all was dark.

Robert Burns (1759–1796)

MAY OF THE MORIL GLEN*

I will tell you of ane wondrous tale,
   As ever was told by man,
Or ever was sung by minstrel meet
   Since this base world began:—

It is of ane May, and ane lovely May,
   That dwelt in the Moril Glen,
The fairest flower of mortal frame,
   But a devil amongst the men;

For nine of them sticket themselves for love,
   And ten louped in the main,
And seven-and-thirty brake their hearts,
   And never loved women again.

For ilk ane trowit she was in love,
   And ran wodde for a while—
There was siccan language in every look,
   And a speire in every smile.

And she had seventy score of ewes,
   That blett o'er dale and down,
On the bonnie braid lands of the Moril Glen,
   And these were all her own;

And she had stotts, and sturdy steers,
   And blithsome kids enew,
That danced as light as gloaming flies
   Out through the falling dew.

And this May she had a snow-white bull,
   The dread of the hail countrye,
And three-and-thretty good milk kye,
   To bear him companye.

And she had geese and goslings too,
   And ganders of muckil din,
And peacocks, with their gaudy trains,
   And hearts of pride within;

And she had cocks with curled kaims,
   And hens, full crouse and glad,
That chanted in her own stack-yard,
   And cackillit and laid like mad.

But where her minnie gat all that gear
   And all that lordly trim,
The Lord in heaven he knew full well,
   But nobody knew but him;

For she never yielded to mortal man,
   To prince, nor yet to king—
She never was given in holy church,
   Nor wedded with ane ring:

So all men wist, and all men said;
   But the tale was in sore mistime,
For a maiden she could hardly be,
   With a daughter in beauty's prime.

But this bonnie May, she never knew
   A father's kindly claim;
She never was bless'd in holy church,
   Nor christen'd in holy name.

But there she lived an earthly flower
   Of beauty so supreme,
Some fear'd she was of the mermaid brood,
   Come out of the salt sea faeme.

Some said she was found in a fairy ring,
   And born of the fairy queen;
For there was a rainbow round the moon
   That night she first was seen.

Some said her mother was a witch,
   Come frae ane far countrye;
Or a princess loved by a weird warlock
   In a land beyond the sea.

O there are doings here below
   That mortal ne'er should ken;
For there are things in this fair world
   Beyond the reach of men!

Ae thing most sure and certain was—
   For the bedesmen told it me—
That the knight who coft the Moril Glen
   Ne'er spoke a word but three.

And the masons who biggit that wild ha' house
   Ne'er spoke word good nor ill;
They came like a dream, and pass'd away
   Like shadows o'er the hill.

They came like a dream, and pass'd away
   Whither no man could tell;
But they ate their bread like Christian men,
   And drank of the crystal well.

And whenever man said word to them,
   They stay'd their speech full soon;
For they shook their heads, and raised their hands,
   And look'd to Heaven aboon.

And the lady came—and there she 'bade
   For mony a lonely day;
But whether she bred her bairn to God
   To read but and to pray—

There was no man wist, though all men guess'd
   And guess'd with fear and dread;
But oh she grew ane virgin rose,
   To seemly womanheid!

And no man could look on her face,
   And eyne that beamed so clear,
But felt a stang gang through his heart,
   Far sharper than a spear;

It was not like ane prodde or pang
   That strength could overwin,
But like ane red hot gaud of iron
   Reeking his heart within.

So that around the Moril Glen
   Our brave young men did lie,
With limbs as lydder, and as lythe,
   As duddis hung out to dry.

And aye the tears ran down in streams
   Ower cheeks right woe-begone;
And aye they gasped, and they gratte,
   And thus made piteous moan:

"Alake that I had ever been born,
   Or dandelit on the knee;
Or rockit in ane cradle bed,
   Beneath a mother's ee!

"Oh! had I died before my cheek
   To woman's breast had lain,
Then had I ne'er for woman's love
   Endured this burning pain!

''For love is like the fiery flame
   That quivers through the rain,
And love is like the pang of death
   That splits the heart in twain.

''If I had loved earthly thing,
   Of earthly blithesomeness,
I might have been beloved again,
   And bathed in earthly bliss.

''But I have loved ane freakish fray
   Of frowardness and sin,
With heavenly beauty on the face,
   And heart of stone within.

''O, for the gloaming calm of death
   To close my mortal day—
The last benighting heave of breath,
   That rends the soul away!''

But word's gone east, and word's gone west,
   'Mong high and low degree,
Quhile it went to the King upon the throne,
   And ane wrothful man was he.—

''What!'' said the king, ''and shall we sit
   In sackcloth mourning sad,
Quhile all mine lieges of the land
   For ane young quean run mad?

''Go saddle me my milk-white steed,
   Of true Megaira brode;
I will go and see this wondrous dame,
   And prove her by the rode.

''And if I find her elfin queen,
   Or thing of fairy kind,
I will burn her into ashes small,
   And sift them on the wind!''

The king hath chosen fourscore knights,
   All busked gallantlye,
And he is away to the Moril Glen,
   As fast as he can dree.

And when he came to the Moril Glen,
   Ae morning fair and clear,
This lovely May on horseback rode
   To hunt the fallow deer.

Her palfry was of snowy hue,—
   A pale unearthly thing
That revell'd over hill and dale,
   Like bird upon the wing.

Her screen was like a net of gold,
   That dazzled as it flew;
Her mantle was of the rainbow's red,
   Her rail of its bonny blue.

A golden comb with diamonds bright,
   Her seemly virgin crown,
Shone like the new moon's lady light
   O'er cloud of amber brown.

The lightning that short from her eyne,
   Flicker'd like elfin brand;
It was sharper nor the sharpest spear
   In all Northumberland.

The hawk that on her bridle arm
   Outspread his pinions blue,
To keep him steady on his perch
   As his loved mistress flew.

Although his een shone like the gleam
   Upon ane sable sea,
Yet to the twain that ower them beam'd,
   Compared they could not be.

Like carry ower the morning sun
   That shimmers to the wind,
So flew her locks upon the gale,
   And streamed afar behind.

The king he wheeled him round about,
   And calleth to his men,
"Yonder she comes, this weirdly witch,
   This spirit of the glen!

"Come, rank your master up behind,
  This serpent to belay;
I'll let you hear me put her down
  In grand polemic way."

Swift came the maid ower strath and stron—
  Nae dantonie dame was she—
Until the king her path withstood,
  In might and majestye.

The virgin cast on him a look,
  With gay and graceful air,
As on some thing below her note,
  That ought not to have been there.

The king, whose belt was like to burst
  With speeches most divine,
Now felt ane throbbing of the heart,
  And quaking of the spine.

And aye he gasped for his breath,
  And gaped in dire dismay,
And waved his arm, and smote his breast,
  But word he could not say.

The spankie grewis they scowr'd the dale
  The dun-deer to restrain;
The virgin gave her steed the rein,
  And followed might and main.

"Go bring her back," the king he cried;
  "This reifery must not be:
Though you should bind her hands and feet,
  Go bring her back to me."

The deer she flew, the garf and grew
  They follow'd hard behind;
The milk-white palfrey brush'd the dew
  Far fleeter nor the wind.

But woe betide the lords and knights,
  That taiglit in the dell!
For though with whip and spur they plied,
  Full far behind they fell.

They look'd outowre their left shoulders,
    To see what they might see,
And there the king in fit of love,
    Lay spurring on the lea.

And aye he battered with his feet,
    And rowted with despair,
And pulled the grass up by the roots,
    And flang it on the air!

"What ails, what ails my royal liege?
    Such grief I do deplore."
"O I'm bewitched," the king replied,
    "And gone for evermore!

"Go bring her back—go bring her back—
    Go bring her back to me;
For I must either die of love,
    Or own that dear ladye!

"That god of love out through my soul
    Hath shot his arrows keen;
And I am enchanted through the heart,
    The liver, and the spleen."

The deer was slain; the royal train
    Then closed the virgin round,
And then her fair and lily hands
    Behind her back were bound.

But who should bind her winsome feet?—
    That bred such strife and pain,
That sixteen brave and belted knights
    Lay gasping on the plain.

And when she came before the king,
    Ane ireful carle was he;
Saith he, "Dame, you must be my love,
    Or burn beneath ane tree.

"For I am so sore in love with thee,
    I cannot go nor stand;
And thinks thou nothing to put down
    The King of fair Scotland?"

"No, I can ne'er be love to thee,
   Nor any lord thou hast;
For you are married men each one,
   And I a maiden chaste.

"But here I promise, and I vow
   By Scotland's king and crown,
Who first a widower shall prove,
   Shall claim me as his own."

The king hath mounted his milk-white steed,—
   One word he said not more—
And he is away from the Moril Glen,
   As ne'er rode king before.

He sank his rowels to the naife,
   And scour'd the muir and dale;
He held his bonnet on his head,
   And louted to the gale,

Till wives ran skreighing to the door,
   Holding their hands on high;
They never saw king in love before,
   In such extremitye.

And every lord and every knight
   Made off his several way,
All galloping as they had been mad,
   Withoutten stop or stay.

But there was never such dool and pain
   In any land befell;
For there is wickedness in man
   That grieveth me to tell.

There was one eye and one alone,
   Beheld the deeds were done;
But the lovely queen of fair Scotland
   Ne'er saw the morning sun;

And seventy-seven wedded dames,
   As fair as e'er were born,
The very pride of all the land,
   Were dead before the morn.

Then there was nought but mourning weeds,
　　And sorrow and dismay;
While burial met with burial still,
　　And jostled by the way.

And graves were howkit in green kirkyards,
　　And howkit deep and wide;
While bedlars swairfit for very toil,
　　The comely corps to hide.

The graves with their unseemly jaws
　　Stood gaping day and night
To swallow up the fair and young;—
　　It was ane grievous sight!

And the bonny May of the Moril Glen
　　Is weeping in despair,
For she saw the hills of fair Scotland
　　Could be her home nae mair.

Then there were chariots came o'er night,
　　As silent and as soon
As shadow of ane little cloud
　　In the wan light of the moon.

Some said they came out of the rock,
　　And some out of the sea;
And some said they were sent from hell,
　　To bring that fair ladye.

When the day sky began to frame
　　The grizly eastern fell,
And the little wee bat was bound to seek
　　His dark and eery cell,

The fairest flower of mortal frame
　　Pass'd from the Moril Glen;
And ne'er may such a deadly eye
　　Shine among Christian men!

James Hogg (1770–1835)

THE WITCH'S BALLAD*

O, I hae come from far away,
  From a warm land far away,
A southern land across the sea,
With sailor-lads about the mast,
Merry and canny, and kind to me.

And I hae been to yon town
  To try my luck in yon town;
Nort, and Mysie, Elspie too.
Right braw we were to pass the gate,
Wi' gowden clasps on girdles blue.

Mysie smiled wi' miminy mouth,
  Innocent mouth, miminy mouth;
Elspie wore a scarlet gown,
Nort's grey eyes were unco gleg.
My Castile comb was like a crown.

We walked abreast all up the street,
  Into the market up the street;
Our hair with marigolds was wound,
Our bodices with love-knots laced,
Our merchandise with tansy bound.

Nort had chickens, I had cocks,
  Gamesome cocks, loud-crowing cocks;
Mysie ducks, and Elspie drakes,—
For a wee groat or a pound;
We lost nae time wi' gives and takes.

Lost nae time, for well we knew,
  In our sleeves full well we knew,
When the gloaming came that night,
Duck nor drake, nor hen nor cock
Would be found by candle-light.

And when our chaffering all was done,
  All was paid for, sold and done,
We drew a glove on ilka hand,
We sweetly curtsied each to each,
And deftly danced a saraband.

The market-lasses looked and laughed,
    Left their gear and looked and laughed;
They made as they would join the game,
But soon their mithers, wild and wud,
With whack and screech they stopped the same.

Sae loud the tongues o' randies grew,
    The flytin' and the skirlin' grew,
At all the windows in the place,
Wi' spoons or knives, wi' needle or awl,
Was thrust out every hand and face.

And down each stair they thronged anon,
    Gentle, semple, thronged anon;
Souter and tailor, frowsy Nan,
The ancient widow young again,
Simpering behind her fan.

Without a choice, against their will,
    Doited, dazed, against their will,
The market lassie and her mither,
The farmer and his husbandman,
Hand in hand dance a' thegither.

Slow at first, but faster soon,
    Still increasing, wild and fast,
Hoods and mantles, hats and hose,
Blindly doffed and cast away,
Left them naked, heads and toes.

They would have torn us limb from limb,
    Dainty limb from dainty limb;
But never one of them could win
Across the line that I had drawn
With bleeding thumb a-widdershin.

But there was Jeff the provost's son,
    Jeff the provost's only son;
There was Father Auld himsel',
The Lombard frae the hostelry,
And the lawyer Peter Fell.

All goodly men we singled out,
    Waled them well, and singled out,

And drew them by the left hand in;
Mysie the priest, and Elspie won
The Lombard, Nort the lawyer carle,
I mysel' the provost's son.

Then, with cantrip kisses seven,
    Three times round with kisses seven,
Warped and woven there spun we
Arms and legs and flaming hair,
Like a whirlwind on the sea.

Like a wind that sucks the sea,
    Over and in and on the sea,
Good sooth it was a mad delight;
And every man of all the four
Shut his eyes and laughed outright.

Laughed as long as they had breath,
    Laughed while they had sense or breath;
And close about us coiled a mist
Of gnats and midges, wasps and flies,
Like the whirlwind shaft it rist.

Drawn up I was right off my feet;
    Into the mist and off my feet;
And, dancing on each chimney-top,
I saw a thousand darling imps
Keeping time with skip and hop.

And on the provost's brave ridge-tile,
    On the provost's grand ridge-tile,
The Blackamoor first to master me
I saw, I saw that winsome smile,
The mouth that did my heart beguile,
And spoke the great Word over me,
In the land beyond the sea.

I called his name, I called aloud,
    Alas! I called on him aloud;
And then he filled his hand with stour,
And he threw it towards me in the air;
My mouse flew out, I lost my pow'r!

My lusty strength, my power were gone;
   Power was gone, and all was gone.
He will not let me love him more!
Of bell and whip and horse's tail
He cares not if I find a store.

But I am proud if he is fierce!
   I am as proud as he is fierce;
I'll turn about and backward go,
If I meet again that Blackamoor,
And he'll help us then, for he shall know
I seek another paramour.

And we'll gang once more to yon town,
   Wi' better luck to yon town;
We'll walk in silk and cramoisie,
And I shall wed the provost's son;
My lady of the town I'll be!

For I was born a crowned king's child,
   Born and nursed a king's child,
King o' a land ayont the sea,
Where the Blackamoor kissed me first,
And taught me art and glamourie.

Each one in her wame shall hide
   Her hairy mouse, her wary mouse,
Fed on madwort and agramie,—
Wear amber beads between her breasts,
And blind-worm's skin about her knee.

The Lombard shall be Elspie's man,
   Elspie's gowden husband-man;
Nort shall take the lawyer's hand;
The priest shall swear another vow,
We'll dance again the saraband!

William Bell Scott (1811–1890)

BRIDE*

O wha's the bride that cairries the bunch
O' thistles blinterin' white?
Her cuckold bridegroom little dreids
What he sall ken this nicht.

For closer than gudeman can come
And closer to 'r than hersel',
Wha didna need her maidenheid
Has wrocht his purpose fell.

O wha 's been here afore me, lass,
And hoo did he get in?
>   —*A man that deed or I was born*
>   *This evil thing has din.*

And left, as it were on a corpse,
Your maidenheid to me?
>   — *Nae lass, gudeman, sin' Time began*
>   *'S hed ony mair to gi'e.*

> *But I can gi'e ye kindness, lad,*
> *And a pair o' willin' hands,*
> *And you sall ha'e my breists like stars,*
> *My limbs like willow wands.*

> *And on my lips ye'll heed nae mair,*
> *And in my hair forget,*
> *The seed o' a' the men that in*
> *My virgin womb ha'e met.*

Hugh MacDiarmid (1892–1978)

THE TRYST*

O luely, luely, cam she in
And luely she lay doun:
I kent her be her caller lips
And her breists sae sma' and roun'.

A' thru the nicht we spak nae word
Nor sinder'd bane frae bane:
A' thru the nicht I heard her hert
Gang soundin' wi' my ain.

It was about the waukrife hour
Whan cocks begin to craw
That she smool'd saftly thru the mirk
Afore the day wud daw.

Sae luely, luely, cam she in
Sae luely was she gaen;
And wi' her a' my simmer days
Like they had never been.

William Soutar (1898–1943)

LOVE IS A GARTH*

Love is a garth whaur lilies are gay
    O pree them early!
And roses brier on the emrod brae
    Sae reid and rarely
To lure the lover's hand to play
    And pree them early.

Love is a garth whaur aipples are fair
    O pree them early!
And cherries jewel the ryces' hair
    Sae reid and rarely
To gar the lover linger there
    And pree them early.

Love is a garth whaur lasses are licht
    O pree them early!
Their lips beglamour the eident sicht
    Sae reid and rarely
To mak the lover lang for nicht
    And pree them early.

Alexander Scott (b. 1920)

MONSTROUS!

Dracula's daughter, Frankenstein's bride,
    Each darling monster maiden,
    On you my love was laden,
Delicious horror's distaff side.

Those babyish blondes who felt your bite
    In throats as pale as skim,
    For me their charm was dim
To the black of your hair and your heart's night.

I feared your fathers, detested your mates
    Who paused in pursuit of redheads
    And spelled you to serve their deadheads—
They ruined our consummation of fates.

Yet still they were always actors only,
    Karloff and Bela Lugosi,
    Familiar familiars, cosy
As country cots no ghost makes lonely.

But you were the nameless nymphs who haunted
    The houses of all my dreams
    With savage sweetness of screams,
Your victim virtue, torn and taunted.

A boy, I loved you, wonderful witches,
    Fated to fail and burn—
    From you I began to learn
To love the world and its terrible riches.

Alexander Scott (b. 1920)

4

Eros Exultant

THE SQUIRE AND THE LADY*

Than unto bed drew everie wicht:
To chalmer went this Ladie bricht,
The quhilk this Squyer did convoy.
Syne, till his bed he went, with joy.
That nicht he sleipit never ane wink,
Bot still did on the Ladie think;
Cupido, with his fyrie dart,
Did peirs him so out throw the hart.
Sa all that nicht he did bot burnit,
Sum tyme sat up, and sumtyme turnit,
Sichand with monie gant and grane,
To fair Venus makand his mane,
Sayand, Ladie, quhat may this mene?
I was ane fre man lait yistrene,
And now ane cative bound and thrall
For ane that I think flour of all.
I pray God sen scho knew my mynd,
How, for hir saik, I am sa pynd.
Wald God I had bene yit in France,
Or I had hapnit sic mischance,
To be subject or serviture
Till ane quhilk takis of me na cure.
This Ladie ludgit neirhand by,
And hard the Squyer prively,
With dreidfull hairt, makand his mone,
With monie cairfull gant and grone.
Hir hart fulfillit with pietie,
Thocht scho wald haif of him mercie,
And said, howbeit I suld be slane,
He sall have lufe for lufe agane.

Wald God I micht, wih my honour,
Have him to be my paramour.
This wes the mirrie tyme of May,
Quhen this fair Ladie, freshe and gay,
Start up, to take the hailsum air,
With pantonis on hir feit ane pair,
Airlie into ane cleir morning,
Befoir fair Phoebus uprysing,
Kirtill alone, withouttin clok,
And saw the Squyeris dure unlok.
Scho slippit in, or ever he wist,
And fenyeitlie past till ane kist,
And with hir keyis oppinnit the lokkis,
And maid hir to take furth ane boxe:
Bot that was not hir erand thair.
With that, this lustie young Squyar
Saw this Ladie so plesantlie
Cum to his chalmer quietlie,
In kyrtill of fyne damais broun,
Hir goldin traissis hingand doun.
Hir pappis were hard, round, and quhyte,
Quhome to behald wes greit delyte.
Lyke the quhyte lyllie wes hir lyre;
Hir hair was like the reid gold wyre;
Hir schankis quhyte withouttin hois,
Quhairat the Squyer did rejois.
And said than, now, vailye quod vailye,
Upon the Ladie thow mak ane sailye.
Hir courtlyk kirtill was unlaist,
And sone into his armis hir braist.
And said to hir; Madame, gude-morne;
Help me, your man that is forlorne.
Without ye mak me sum remeid,
Withouttin dout I am bot deid;
Quhairfoir, ye mon releif my harmes.
With that, he hint hir in his armes,
And talkit with hir on the flure;
Syne, quyetlie did bar the dure.
Squyer (quod scho) quhat is your will?
Think ye my womanheid to spill?
Na, God forbid, it wer greit syn;
My Lord and ye wes neir of kyn.
Quhairfoir, I mak yow supplicatioun,
Pas, and seik ane dispensatioun;

Than sall I wed yow with ane ring;
Than may ye leif at your lyking.
For ye are young, lustie, and fair,
And als ye ar your fatheris air.
Thair is na ladie, in all this land,
May yow refuse to hir husband;
And gif ye lufe me as ye say,
Haist to dispens the best ye may;
And thair to yow I geve my hand,
I sall yow tak to my husband.
(Quod he) quhill that I may indure,
I vow to be your serviture;
Bot I think greit vexatioun
To tarie upon dispensatioun.
Than in his armis he did hir thrist,
And aither uther sweitlie kist,
And wame for wame thay uther braissit;
With that, hir kirtill wes unlaissit.
Than Cupido, with his fyrie dartis,
Inflammit sa thir luiferis hartis,
Thay micht na maner of way dissever,
Nor ane micht not part fra ane uther;
Bot, like wodbind, thay wer baith wrappit.
Thair tenderlie he hes hir happit,
Full softlie up, intill his bed.
Judge ye gif he hir schankis shed.
Allace (quod scho) quhat may this mene?
And with hir hair scho dicht hir ene.
I can not tell how thay did play;
Bot I beleve scho said not nay.
He pleisit hir sa, as I hard sane,
That he was welcum ay agane.
Scho rais, and tenderlie him kist,
And on his hand ane ring scho thrist;
And he gaif hir ane lufe drowrie,
Ane ring set with ane riche rubie,
In takin that thair lufe for ever
Suld never frome thir twa dissever.
And than scho passit unto hir chalmer,
And fand hir madinnis, sweit as lammer,
Sleipand full sound; and nothing wist
How that thair Ladie past to the kist.
(Quod thay) Madame, quhair have ye bene?
(Quod scho) into my gardine grene,

To heir thir mirrie birdis sang.
I lat yow wit, I thocht not lang,
Thocht I had taryit thair quhill none.
(Quod thai) quhair wes your hois and schone?
Quhy gied ye with your bellie bair?
(Quod scho) the morning wes sa fair:
For, be him that deir Jesus sauld,
I felt na wayis ony maner of cauld.
(Quod thay) Madame, me think ye sweit.
(Quod scho) ye see I sufferit heit;
The dew did sa on flouris fleit,
That baith my lymmis ar maid weit:
Thairfoir ane quhyle I will heir ly,
Till this dulce dew be fra me dry.

Sir David Lyndsay (1486–1555)

MY HAIRT IS HEICH*

My hairt is heich aboif, my body is full of blis,
for I am sett in lufe als weill as I wald wis.
I lufe my lady pure and scho luvis me agane,
I am hir serviture, scho is my soverane,
scho is my verry harte, I am her howp and heill,
scho is my joy inwart, I am hir luvar leill,
I am hir bound and thrall, scho is at my command,
I am perpetuall hir man both fute and hand.
The thing that may hir pleis, my body sall fulfill;
quhat evir hir diseis, it dois my body ill.
My bird, my bony ane, my tendir bab venust,
my lufe, my life allane, my liking and my lust,
we interchange our hairtis in utheris armis soft,
spreitless we twa depertis, usand our luvis oft:
we murne quhen licht day dawis, we plene the nycht is schort,
we curs the cok that crawis that hinderis our disport.
I glowffin up agast quhen I hir mys on nycht
and in my oxster fast I find the bowster richt.
Than langour on me lyis, lyk Morpheus, the mair,
quhilk causis me uprys and to my sweit repair,
and than is all the sorrow furth of remembrance
that evir I had a forrow in luvis observance.
Thus nevir I do rest, so lusty a life I leid
quhen that I list to test the well of womanheid.

Luvaris in pane, I pray God send you sic remeid
as I haif nycht and day, you to defend frome deid.
Thairfoir be evir trew unto your ladeis fre
and thay will on you rew, as mine hes done one me.

Anonymous (16th century)

UP, HELSUM HAIRT*

Up, helsum hairt, thy rutis rais and lowp,
exalt and clym within my breist in staige.
Art thou not wantoun, haill and in gud howp,
fermit in grace and fre of all thirlaige,
bathing in blis and sett in hie curaige,
braisit in joy? No falt may thee affray,
having thy ladeis hart as heretaige
in blenche ferme for ane sallat every May.
So neidis thou nocht now sussy, sytt nor sorrow,
sen thou art sure of sollace evin and morrow.

Thou, Cupeid king, rewardit me with this.
I am thy awin trew liege without tressone.
Thair levis no man in moir eis, welth and blis.
I knaw no siching, sadness nor yit soun,
walking, thocht, langour, lamentatioun,
dolor, dispair, weiping nor jelosye.
My breist is void and purgit of pussoun.
I feill no pane. I haif no purgatorye,
bot peirles, perfytt, paradisall plesour,
with mirry hairt and mirthfulnes but mesoure.

My lady, lord, thou gaif me for to hird,
Within mine armes I nureis on the nycht.
Kissing, I say "My bab, my tendir bird,
sweit maistres, lady luffe and lusty wicht,
steir, rewll and gyder of my sensis richt."
My voice surmontis the sapheir cludis hie,
thanking grit God of that tressour and micht.
I coft hir deir, bot scho fer derrer me,
quhilk hasard honor, fame in aventeur,
committing clene hir corse to me in cure.

Scotch Passion

In oxteris clois we kis and cossis hairtis,
brynt in desire of amouris play and sport,
meittand oure lustis. Spreitles we twa depertis.
Prolong with lasir, lord, I thee exhort,
sic time that we may boith tak our confort,
first for to sleip, syne walk without espyis.
I blame the cok. I plene the nicht is schort.
Away I went. My wache the cuschett cryis,
wissing all luvaris leill to haiff sic chance
that thay may haif us in remembrance.

Alexander Scott (c. 1515–c. 1583)

BLEST*

Blest, blest and happy he
Whose eyes behold her face,
But blessed more whose ears hath heard
The speeches framed with grace

And he is half a god
That these thy lips may kiss,
Yet god all whole that may enjoy
    Thy body as it is.

Anonymous (17th century)

SHE ROSE AND LET ME IN*

The night her sable mantle wore,
    And gloomy were the skies,
Of glittering stars appeared no more
    Than those in Nelly's eyes.
When at her father's yett I knocked,
    When I had often been,
She, shrouded only in her smock,
    Arose and let me in.

Fast locked within her close embrace,
    She trembling stood, ashamed;
Her swelling breast and glowing face
    And every touch inflamed.

My eager passion I obeyed,
  Resolved the fort to win,
And her fond heart was soon betrayed
  To yield and let me in.

Then, then, beyond expressing,
  Transporting was the joy,
I knew no greater blessing,
  So blest a man was I;
And she, all ravished with delight,
  Bid me oft come again,
And kindly vowed that every night
  She'd rise and let me in.

Francis Semple (c. 1616–1682)

POLWART ON THE GREEN

At Polwart on the Green
If you'll meet me the morn,
Where lasses do conveen
To dance about the thorn;
A kindly welcome you shall meet
  Frae her wha likes to view
A lover and a lad complete,
  The lad and lover you.

Let dorty dames say Na,
As lang as e'er they please,
Seem caulder than the sna',
While inwardly they bleeze;
But I will frankly shaw my mind,
  And yield my heart to thee;
Be ever to the captive kind,
  That langs na to be free.

At Polwart on the Green,
Amang the new-maun hay,
With sangs and dancing keen
We'll pass the heartsome day,
At night, if beds be o'er thrang laid,
  And thou be twin'd of thine,
Thou shalt be welcome, my dear lad,
  To take a part of mine.

Allan Ramsay (1686–1758)

KISSED YESTREEN

Kiss'd yestreen, and kiss'd yestreen,
Up the Gallowgate, down the Green:
I've woo'd wi' lords, and woo'd wi' lairds,
I've mooled wi' carles and mell'd wi' cairds,
I've kiss'd wi' priests—'twas done i' the dark,
Twice in my gown and thrice in my sark;
But priest, nor lord, nor loon can gie
Sic kindly kisses as he gae me.

Anonymous (18th century)

THE FORNICATOR*

Ye jovial boys who love the joys,
    The blissful joys of Lovers;
Yet dare avow with dauntless brow,
    When th' bony lass discovers;
I pray draw near and lend an ear,
    And welcome in a Frater,
For I've lately been on quarantine,
    A proven Fornicator.

Before the Congregation wide
    I pass'd the muster fairly,
My handsome Betsey by my side,
    We gat our ditty rarely;
But my downcast eye by chance did spy
    What made my lips to water,
Those limbs so clean where I, between,
    Commenc'd a Fornicator.

With rueful face and signs of grace
    I pay'd the buttock-hire,
The night was dark and thro' the park
    I could not but convoy her;
A parting kiss, what could I less,
    My vows began to scatter,
My Betsey fell—lal de lal lal lal,
    I am a Fornicator.

But for her sake this vow I make,
   And solemnly I swear it,
That while I own a single crown,
   She's welcome for to share it;
And my roguish boy his Mother's joy,
   And the darling of his Pater,
For him I boast my pains and cost,
   Although a Fornicator.

Ye wenching blades whose hireling jades
   Have tipt you off blue-boram,
I tell ye plain, I do disdain
   To rank you in the Quorum;
But a bony lass upon the grass
   To teach her esse Mater,
And no reward but for regard,
   O that 's a Fornicator.

Your warlike Kings and Heros bold,
   Great Captains and Commanders,
Your might Cesars fam'd of old,
   And Conquering Alexanders;
In fields they fought and laurels bought
   And bulwarks strong did batter,
But still they grac'd our noble list
   And ranked Fornicator!!!

Robert Burns (1759–1796)

THE RANTIN DOG*

O Wha my babie-clouts will buy,
O Wha will tent me when I cry;
Wha will kiss me where I lie,
The rantin dog the daddie o't.

O Wha will own he did the faut,
O Wha will buy the groanin maut,
O Wha will tell me what to ca 't,
The rantin dog the daddie o't.

When I mount the Creepie-chair,
Wha will set beside me there,

Gie me Rob, I'll seek nae mair,
The rantin dog the daddie o't.

Wha will crack to me my lane;
Wha will mak me fidgin fain;
Wha will kiss me o'er again
The rantin dog the daddie o't.

Robert Burns (1759–1796)

LIBEL SUMMONS*

In Truth and Honour's name—AMEN—
Know all men by these Presents plain:—
This fourth o' June, at Mauchline given,
The year 'tween eighty-five and seven,
WE, Fornicators by profession,
As per extractum from each Session,
In way and manner here narrated,
Pro bono Amor congregated;
And by our brethren constituted,
A COURT OF EQUITY deputed.—
With special authoris'd direction
To take beneath our strict protection
The stays-out-bursting quondam maiden,
With GROWING LIFE and anguish laden;
Who by the rascal is deny'd,
That led her thoughtless steps aside.—
He who disowns the ruin'd Fair-one,
And for her wants and woes does care none;
The wretch that can refuse subsistence
To those whom he has given existence;
He who when at a lass's by-job,
Defrauds her with a fr-g or dry-b-b;
The coof that stands on clishmaclavers
When women hafflins offer favors:—
All who in any way or manner
Distain the Fornicator's honor,
We take cognisance thereananent,
The proper Judges competent.—

First, POET B——s he takes the chair,
Allow'd by a', his title 's fair;
And pass'd nem. con. without dissension,

He has a DUPLICATE pretension.—
Next, Merchant SMITH, our worthy FISCAL,
To cow each pertinaceous rascal;
In this, as every other state,
His merit is conspicuous great:
RICHMOND the third, our trusty CLERK,
The minutes regular to mark,
And sit dispenser of the law,
In absence of the former twa;
The fourth our MESSENGER AT ARMS,
When failing all the milder terms,
HUNTER, a hearty, willing brother,
Weel skill'd in dead and living leather.—
Without PREAMBLE less or more said,
We, body politic aforesaid,
With legal, due WHEREAS, and WHEREFORE,
We are appointed here to care for
The interests of our constituents,
And punish contraveening truants,
Keeping a proper regulation
Within the lists of FORNICATION.—

WHEREAS, our FISCAL, by petition,
Informs us there is strong suspicion,
You, Coachman DOW, and Clockie BROWN,
Baith residenters in this town;
In other words, you, JOCK, and, SANDY,
Hae been at wark at HOUGHMAGANDIE;
And now when facts are come to light,
The matter ye deny outright.—

FIRST, YOU, JOHN BROWN, there's witness borne,
And affidavit made and sworn,
That ye hae bred a hurly-burly
'Bout JEANY MITCHEL's tirlie-whirlie,
And blooster'd at her regulator,
Till a' her wheels gang clitter-clatter.—
And farther still, ye cruel Vandal,
A tale might even in hell be scandal!
That ye hae made repeated trials
Wi' drugs and draps in doctor's phials,
Mixt, as ye thought, wi' fell infusion,
Your ain begotten wean to poosion.—
And yet ye are sae scant o' grace,

Ye daur to lift your brazen face,
And offer for to take your aith,
Ye never lifted JEANY's claith.—
But tho' ye should yoursel manswear,
Laird Wilson's sclates can witness bear,
Ae e'ening of a MAUCHLINE fair,
That JEANY's masts they saw them bare;
For ye had furl'd up her sails,
And was at play—at heads and tails.—

Next, SANDY DOW, you're here indicted
To have, as publickly you're wyted,
Been clandestinely upward whirlin
The petticoats o' MAGGY BORELAN,
And giein her canister a rattle,
That months to come it winna settle.—
And yet, ye offer your protest,
Ye never herried Maggy's nest;
Tho', it's weel ken'd that at her gyvel
Ye hae gien mony a kytch and kyvel.—

Then BROWN and DOW, before design'd,
For clags and clauses there subjoin'd,
We, COURT aforesaid, cite and summon,
That on the fifth o' July comin,
The hour o' cause, in our Court-ha',
At Whitefoord's arms, ye answer LAW!

BUT, as reluctantly we PUNISH,
An' rather, mildly would admonish:
Since Better PUNISHMENT prevented,
Than OBSTINACY sair repented.—

THEN, for that ANCIENT SECRET'S SAKE,
You have the honor to partake;
An' for that NOBLE BADGE you wear,
YOU, SANDIE DOW, our BROTHER dear,
We give you as a MAN an' MASON
This private, sober, friendly lesson.—

YOUR CRIME, a manly deed we view it,
As MAN ALONE, can only do it;
But, in denial persevering,
Is to a SCOUNDREL'S NAME adhering.

The BEST O' MEN, hae been surpris'd;
The BEST O' WOMEN been advis'd:
NAY, CLEVEREST LADS hae haen a TRICK O'T,
AN', BONNIEST LASSES taen a LICK O'T.—

Then Brother Dow, if you're asham'd
In such a QUORUM to be nam'd,
Your conduct much is to be blam'd.
See, ev'n HIMSEL—there's GODLY BRYAN,
The auld WHATRECK he has been tryin;
When such as he put to their han',
What man on CHARACTER need stan'?
Then Brother dear, lift up your brow,
And, like yoursel, the TRUTH avow;
Erect a dauntless face upon it,
An' say, "I am the man has done it;
"I SANDIE DOW GAT MEG WI' WEAN,
"An 's fit to do as much again."
Ne'er mind their solemn rev'rend faces,
Had they—in proper times an' places,
But SEEN AN' FUN'—I mukle dread it,
They just would done as you an' WE did.—
TO TELL THE TRUTH 's a manly lesson,
An' doubly proper in A MASON.

YOU MONSIEUR BROWN, as it is proven,
JEAN MITCHEL's wame by you was hoven;
Without you by a quick repentance
Acknowledge Jean's an' your acquaintance,
Depend on't, this shall be your sentence.—
Our beadles to the Cross shall take you,
And there shall mither naked make you;
Some canie grip near by your middle,
They shall it bind as tight 's a fiddle;
The raep they round the PUMP shall tak
An' tye your hands behint your back;
Wi' just an ell o' string allow'd
To jink an' hide you frae the croud:
There ye shall stan', a legal seizure,
In during Jeanie Mitchel's pleasure;
So be, her pleasure dinna pass
Seven turnings of a half-hour glass:
Nor shall it in her pleasure be
To louse you out in less than THREE.—

THIS, our futurum esse DECREET,
We mean it not to keep a secret;
But in OUR SUMMONS here insert it,
And whoso dares, may controvert it.—

THIS, mark'd before the date and place is,
SIGILLUM EST, PER,
              B---S THE PRESES.

This Summons and the signet mark,
EXTRACTUM EST, PER.
              RICHMOND, CLERK.

AT MAUCHLINE, idem date of June,
'Tween six and seven, the afternoon,
You twa, in propria personae,
Within design'd, SANDY and JOHNY,
This SUMMONS legally have got,
As vide witness underwrote:
Within the house of JOHN DOW, vintner.
NUNC FACIO HOC,
              GULLELMUS HUNTER.

Robert Burns (1759–1796)

NOW BARE TO THE BEHOLDER'S EYE

Now bare to the beholder's eye
Your late denuded lendings lie,
Subsiding slowly where they fell,
A disinvested citadel;
The obdurate corset, Cupid's foe,
The Dutchman's breeches frilled below,
Hose that the lover loves to note,
And white and crackling petticoat.

From these, that on the ground repose,
Their lady lately re-arose;
And laying by the lady's name
A living woman re-became.
Of her, that from the public eye
They do inclose and fortify,
Now, lying scattered as they fell

An indiscreeter tale they tell:
Of that more soft and secret her
Whose daylong fortresses they were,
By fading warmth, by lingering print,
These now discarded scabbards hint.

A twofold change the ladies know.
First, in the morn the bugles blow,
And they, with floral hues and scents,
Man their be-ribboned battlements.
But let the stars appear, and they
Shed inhumanities away;
And from the changeling fashion sees,
Through comic and through sweet degrees,
In nature's toilet unsurpassed,
Forth leaps the laughing girl at last.

Robert Louis Stevenson (1850–1894)

THE FINE FECHTIN MOOSE*

"Fairest o' fair, O hear my cry;
O, open and let your love inby;
Sae lang have I been here standin,
 Ay, ay, ay standin,
That I'm frozen all-utterly."

"Deed, and I winna open to ye,
Nor to ony gangrel, as weel ye may be;
But first, you maun tell me strauchtly,
 Ay, ay, ay, strauchtly,
That there's nane that you lo'e but me."

"Dear lass, I lo'e you; weel you ken
That you've aye been the only ane.
But sae lang have I been here standin,
 Ay, ay, ay, standin,
That I'm frozen cauld to the bane."

In the nicht, in the nicht, in the middle o' the nicht,
A dunt at the winnock gae's baith a fricht.
And her mither, O ay, *she* heard it,
 Ay, ay, ay, SHE heard it:
"Are you sure, Jean, that a' thing's a' richt?"

"O mither, it's only Baudrons, the cat:
He's efter a moose, and that's what he's at;
And dod, but he's grippit the beastie;
  Ay, ay, ay, the beastie—
She's a fine fechtin moose for a' that."

                                    Sir Alexander Gray (1882–1968)

SERVANT GIRL'S BED

The talla spales
And the licht loups oot,
Fegs, it's your ain creesh
Lassie, I doot,
And the licht that reeled
Loose on't a wee
Was the bonny lowe
O' Eternity.

                                    Hugh MacDiarmid (1892–1978)

SOLIPSIST*

My white lass wi the een o a fawn,
Straucht here by me on the gerss
Whar aa the world is skrucken
  Til this wee gair
Mune-shadawed by a runkelt tree
  In Cynthia's nicht
  O' siller glamourie—
Your hair a midnicht forest
  Thrang
    Wi the greitan dirl,
The schere sang-spate o rossignels—
  While the great gowden ernes
  That rule my saul
  Like princes o the bluid
Scove throu the thrawan hairns
On what fell errand I ken nocht—
  Nor you, my ain, my sleepan,
    Saft, born-skaithit hert.

Here aa the world is this wee gair
We hap nou wi our bodies' length
Thegither as we were but ane
—"The twa-backit beast"! I ken—
    —But mair is twafauld nor the beast:
The Beautie that the Beast maun bed
  Is twafauld here, the Fairheid
  O' our luve, and twafauld tae
  Is aa that ee can see;
The yerth is us, the lift, the mune,
Aa couplit in our couplin here,
And there is nocht but our twa sels,
Our passion's gleid, our herts, our sauls,
Ablow, aben, ayont, abune—
My luve that aince I had—and tint.

—As sayis the auntient Catechist:
"Luve is the great Solipsist."

(Verb. Sap.)
Sydney Goodsir Smith (1915–1975)

DA SIMPLE LIFE*
(*From the French of Villon*)

Incooched in silken doon, a boordly priest,
Warmin his hams afore a fire's het gloed,
Wi lovely Leddy Sonia lyin neist,
Souple an scentit, white save whaar da bloed
At coorsed oonseen her smooth limbs raise in floed
An dyed her velvet sheek an crimson lips,
Pairted ta laach an kyiss, as fast he clips
Her sweet bare breest an coels his boady's strife:
Dan kent I, skoitin whaar da coortin slips,
Dir no a traisir laek an aisy life.

If Frank Gontier and Helen, his helpmate,
Hed tried dis jantil life, A'll gie my aith
Dan wid dey no hae been sae glig ta aet
Aingins an moericks at mak strang da braith.
Dir stap an liver-muggies, hamespun claith,
I haaldna wirt a strae. Dey mak a sang
Becaas dey boel dir boadies doon amang

Da heddir-cowes. Whaar wid ye reddir swife,
Abrod or warm abed? What, tink ye lang?
Dir no a traisir laek an aisy life.

Dey live on coorse black bread o aets an bere;
Caald watter swills it doon da hale year roond.
I widna live a day on sic poer fare—
No, nor a moarnin. Whaar da burn is crooned
Wi boanie briars, Frank has his Nellie dooned,
Her back well-shoardit wi twa-faald o plaid,
An taks his plaisir on a caald aert bed.
A'm weel contentit, sin A'm no his wife;
Bit what so e'er ye tink of Love's hard tred,
Dir no a traisir laek an aisy life.

O Prince, judge noo an mak wis aa agree,
For A'm no een wid stir up ony strife;
Bit whin a bairn, dey affen said ta me:
Dir no a traisir laek an aisy life.

William J. Tait (b. 1918)

FROM A CITY BALCONY

How often when I think of you the day grows bright!
Our silent love
wanders in Glen Fruin with butterflies and cuckoos—
bring me the drowsy country thing! Let it drift above the traffic
by the open window with a cloud of witnesses—
a sparkling burn, white lambs, the glaze of gorse,
the cuckoos calling madly, the real white clouds over us,
white butterflies about your hand in the short hot grass,
and then the witness was my hand closing on yours,
my mouth brushing your eyelids and your lips
again and again till you sighed and turned for love.
Your breasts and thighs were blazing like the gorse.
I covered your great fire in silence there.
We let the day grow old among the grass.
It was in the silence the love was.

Footsteps and witnesses! In this Glasgow balcony who pours
such joy like mountain water? It brims, it spills over and over
down to the parched earth and the relentless wheels.

How often will I think of you, until
our dying steps forget this light, forget
that we ever knew the happy glen,
or that I ever said, We must jump into the sun,
and we jumped into the sun.

Edwin Morgan (b. 1920)

COVER GIRL

From the enfillade of her eyes,
the encirclement of her arms,
the charge of her breasts,
the envelopment of her hips,
the pincer-moves of her thighs,
her total onslaught—

No cover.

Alexander Scott (b. 1920)

PERSONAL COLUMN

In daydream fantasies of self-indulgence
my favourite theme is the scene where
I walk into a room loaded with innocence
to be the victim of an orgy there.

The background varies, but my home will do,
where I am greeted by five lady guests,
or a strange hotel, a midnight interview:
and I gasp helpless under dabbling breasts.

Why do I stage intrigues of such dimension,
always eager to be outnumbered in the deed?
For the carnal fact is, I hasten to mention,
that I would never deny a lady in need.

When Ladies' Circles invite me to remote spots,
I accept with alacrity and warm suspicion.
I leave my door unlocked and cook in my thoughts,
but not one nymphomaniac seeks admission.

So damn all those lousy novelists who instil
sex as a fillip, larkin' around like fizz,
which makes one hanker for the pay-off thrill:
a little taste of how Orpheus got his.

                                                    W. Price Turner (b. 1927)

LETTER FROM A PARTISAN

Up here in the orgone stream our muscular
armour relaxes com-
pletely, pinetrees shimmy
like dildos on their moist pelvic
floor and oxygenated water
cascades past our sensitized ears.

In our mountain command post
our synapses are in full spasm suffused
with invisible telepathic
vibrations as we plan the lib-
eration of Scotland
from the puritanical conformist unionist hordes.

Our cap-
tain (confined to his sleeping-bag
with a painful bout of genital
cramp) issues his orders in curt quiet tones:
you can hear the copper clunk of bullets, the plop
of rain on a mapcase.

Message boys slip away through the bracken
to contact our suburban groupuscules: they
travel on foot hitching occasional lifts
from unsuspecting lairds and suspicious ministers
stopping only at lonely Highland mo-
tels for a lay and a sip of the cratur.

At the head of the Black
Loch we ambush a file of artificial insemination
technologists. We entertain com-
rades from Truro—for them
our uniformed girls open their soft
parts as a gesture of interfraternal sol-

idarity. We question an agent
provocateur from St Andrews House nearly
yanking his balls off. It's a hard
life but a good one
up here in the mountains. Tell Charlie
thanks for the truss. Scotland for ever!

Tom Buchan (b. 1931)

EDINBURGH SCENE

we used to be typists
but the hell wi' that
now we live with these boys
in a two room flat

we've never washed for ages
we sleep on bits of sack
we've baith lost wir pants
and we dinnae want them back

the boys are a' big beardies
they think we're awfy sweet
we never know which one we're with
that's what it means to be beat

Alan Jackson (b. 1938)

THE BLACK JUDGE DEBONAIR

A blonde with great legendary eyes flew down,
Lit nestling on the bar-stool. I
Ordered her a cursory martini and
Turned to resume our talk, but the dark judge was
Already at her other wing, faking profound
Fellow-feeling.

Relish for the pub's decor,
Delight in the plosive froth, and a gleaming wit
About fishnet stockings brought him close to the bull's-eye.
Her giggling and readjustment on the stool
Sighted his aim.

      And it was not closing time
That took them from the pub, and led them down
To the open allotment gardens, under the grey
Starlight.

      As he undid her out of zips
And hooks the night
Was innumerably still. He slipped off his own
Clothes and laid her down along the verge
And all laughter was gone from her features. After a certain point
The inadequacy of facial expression is best
Masked altogether. He stood back
To admire his work, God on a seventh day
Hanging above action. And saw the red
Judge's grin absent from the factual target.

That calm godlikeness in the upper air
Shatters, and is more a hawk that
Stoops furiously onto its simple prey.

                             David Black (b. 1941)

THE REALM OF TOUCHING

Between my lips the taste of night-time blends
And then dissolves. It is blank as my eyelids close.
For a flickering of time I concentrate on how time ends.

It should be present, the scent of the rose
We bought, though one petal has begun to fall.
Somehow that simplifies the girl I chose.

Night music must be the sweetest sound of all.
It is made to overwhelm with virtuosity.
But every night it is the same pounding on the same wall.

Nocturnal images are said to be the ones that stay
Longest, with exploitation of the dark half-tone.
This I disregard and watch for the day.

A touch in the realm of touching alone
Adds presence to the absence of light.

A clasp of hands, then bodies, my own
And hers is when I welcome the blindness of night.

Alan Bold (b. 1943)

SAPPER

Yard by yard I let you
sap my resistance
and undermine
my easy independence.

Your smiles and warm ways
burrowed burning
into my cool brain; your firmness
honeycombed my heart.

Then you laid in
barrel-loads of love
and laid a powder trail
to the ammunition dump

of my desire. And now
I've caught you, hand
on my fuse. And I say
"Yes, love."

Andrew Greig (b. 1951)

5

Eros Enraptured

LOVE AT FIRST SIGHT*

And therewith kest I doune myn eye ageyne
Quhare as I saw walking under the toure,
Full secretly new cummyn hir to pleyne,
The fairest or the freschest yong floure
That ever I sawe, me thought, before that houre;
For quhich sodayne abate anone astert
The blude of all my body to my hert.

And though I stude abaisit tho alyte,
No wonder was, for quhy my wittis all
Were so ouercome with plesance and delyte,
Onely throu latting of myn eyen fall,
That sudaynly my hert become hir thrall
For ever of free wyll, for of manace
There was no takyn in her suete face.

And in my hede I drew ryght hastily,
And eftsones I lent it forth ageyne
And sawe hir walk, that verray womanly,
With no wight mo bot onely women tweyne.
Than gan I studye in my self and seyne:
"A, swete, are ye a warldly creature,
Or hevinly thing in liknesse of nature? . . ."

Quhen I a lytill thrawe had maid my moon,
Bewailing myn infortune and my chance,
Unknawin how or quhat was best to doon,
So ferre I fallyng was in lufis dance
That sodeynly my wit, my contenance,
My hert, my will, my nature and my mynd,
Was changit clene ryght in ane othir kynd.

Off hir array the forme gif I sall write,
Toward hir goldin haire and riche atyre,
It fret-wise couchit was with perllis quhite
And grete balas lemyng as the fyre,
With mony ane emeraut and fair saphire,
And on hir hede a chaplet fresche of hewe,
Off plumys partit rede and quhite and blewe;

All full of quaking spangis bryght as gold,
Forgit of schap like to the amorettis,
So new, so fresch, so plesant to behold;
The plumys eke like to the floure jonettis
And othir of schap like to the margarettis,
And above all this there was, wele I wote,
Beautee eneuch to mak the world to dote;

About hir neck, quhite as the fyne amaille
A gudely cheyne of smale orfeverye,
Quhareby there hang a ruby without faille,
Lyke to ane herte schapin verily,
That as a sperk of love so wantounly
Semyt birnyng upon hir quhyte throte.
Now, gif there was gud partye, god it wote!

And for to walk that fresche mayes morowe
Ane huke sche had upon hir tissew quhite,
That gudeliar had nought bene sene toforowe
As I suppose, and girt sche was alyte.
Thus haflyng louse for haste, to suich delyte
It was to see hir youth in gudelihed,
That for rudenes to speke thereof I drede.

In hir was youthe, beautee, with humble aport,
Bountee, richesse and wommanly facture,
God better wote than my pen can report,
Wisedome, largesse, estate and connyng sure.
In every poynt so guydit hir mesure,
In word, in dede, in schap, in contenance,
That nature myght no more hir childe avance.

Throw quich anone I knew and understude
Wele that sche was a warldly creature;
On quhom to rest myn eye, so mich gude
It did my wofull hert, I yow assure,
That it was to me joye without mesure . . .

King James I (1394–1437)

SO SWEET A KISS

So swete a kis yistrene fra thee I reft,
In bowing down thy body on the bed,
That evin my lyfe within thy lippis I left;
Sensyne from thee my spirits wald never shed;
To folow thee it from my body fled,
And left my corps als cold as ony kie.
But when the danger of my death I dred,
To seik my spreit I sent my harte to thee;
Bot it wes so inamored with thyn ee,
With thee it myndit likwyse to remane:
So thou hes keept captive all the thrie,
More glaid to byde then to returne agane.
Except thy breath thare places had suppleit,
Even in thyn armes, thair doutles had I deit.

Alexander Montgomerie (c. 1545–c. 1610)

DREAM

I dreamit ane dreame, o that my dreame wer trew!
Me thocht my maistris to my chalmer came,
And with hir harmeles handis the cowrteingis drew,
And suetlie callit on me be my name:
"Art ye on sleip," quod sche, "o fy for shame!
Have ye nocht tauld that luifaris takis no rest?"
Me thocht I ansuerit, "trew it is, my dame,
I sleip nocht, so your luif dois me molest."
With that me thocht hir nicht-gowne of sche cuist,
Liftit the claiss and lichtit in my armis;
Hir Rosie lippis me thocht on me sche thirst,
And said, "may this nocht stanche yow of your harmes!"
"Mercy, madame," me thocht I menit to say,
Bot quhen I walkennit, alace, sche wes away.

Alexander Montgomerie (c. 1545–c. 1610)

WHEESHT, WHEESHT

Wheesht, wheesht, my foolish hert,
For weel ye ken
I widna ha'e ye stert
Auld ploys again.

It's guid to see her lie
Sae snod an' cool,
A' lust o' lovin' by—
Wheesht, wheesht, ye fule!

Hugh MacDiarmid (1892–1978)

BIRTH OF A GENIUS AMONG MEN

The night folded itself about me like a woman's hair.
Thousands of dispersed forces drawn as by a magnet
Streamed through the open windows—millions of stars poured through;
What destiny were they seeking in us, what outlet?

An immense vigour awoke in my body.
My breast expanded and overflowed into the night.
I was one with Scotland out there and with all the world
And thoughts of your beauty shone in me like starlight.

You were all female, ripe as a rose for my plucking.
I was all male and no longer resisted my need.
The earth obeyed the rhythm of our panting.
The mountains sighed with us. Infinity was emptied.

To both of us it seemed as if we had never loved before.
A miracle was abroad and I knew that not merely I
Had accomplished the act of love but the whole universe through me,
A great design was fulfilled, another genius nigh.

Yet I lay awake and as the daylight broke
I heard the faint voices of the Ideas discuss
The way in which they could only express themselves yet
In fragmentary and fallacious forms through us.

Hugh MacDiarmid (1892–1978)

MY WEIRD IS COMFORTED*
(*From the medieval Latin*)

My weird is comforted by singin
Juist like a swan when Daith comes stingin
Nae colour to my face is springin
But dolour in my breist is dingin

Care nevir crynin
Smeddum fast dwynin
Darg has me pynin
In dule I die
I die, I die, I die
The while my love cares nocht for me.

Gif she to my desire wad listen
I wadna caa the king my cuisin
She'd share her bed and gie her blissin
Her lips be mine alane for kissin
I'd meet Daith crousely
Depairt life sprucely
Submittin doucely
For sic employ
T'enjoy, enjoy, enjoy
And nocht could my delyte destroy.

While on her bosom I am thinkin
I wad my haun were there to sink in
Frae pap to pap gae fondly linkin.
The thochts that through my heid are jinkin!
In shyness or shamin
Her rosy mou's flamin
Alowe I am claimin
Her lips to pree
And pree and pree and pree
And leave my mark for aa to see.

J. K. Annand (b. 1908)

DIALOGUE AT MIDNIGHT

C ome ben, my dear, she said, and lie
I n my airms sae white and cool—
C an man, I spiert, his saul no flee
E lse but in drink and lecherie?—
L eman, leman, thochts are fules;
Y our saul sleeps atween my thies.

Sydney Goodsir Smith (1915–1975)

THESE TWO LOVERS

At any moment of the day
you'll suddenly turn to me and say,
"Tell me you love me." So I do.
Yet, as I pass the words to you,
sometimes, preoccupied, my nuance
seems to deny you the assurance
you need so urgently. And I
find myself challenged to deny
the opposite of what I mean.
A sightless distance blurts between
us two, and I then re-discover
how islanded is loved from lover.

When all pretensions are unmade
and we together lie in bed
as lovers do, our bodies' act
renews the temporary pact
that shores a little warming grace
from the cold wash of nothingness.
But though you curl into my side,
fulfilled and sleepy, the divide
that mists us all, swirls back, and I
watch the Plough rust against the sky,
the sense of person and of place
sieved through the fall-away of space.

Until, unconsciously, you press
my hand against your nakedness.
Pulling me back to now and here,
you narrow distance from my fear.
I feel your breathing, and am sure
however torn and insecure
the lineaments of human trust,
our bodies' simple touching lust
tautens a wholeness running through
the variants of me and you,
so turn to sleep; like you, content
should this togetherness we're lent
prove to be all that living meant.

Maurice Lindsay (b. 1918)

NAMELESS

You step from underthings,
lie down beside me.
What we touch is earth
parched with explanation.

Rain over Eden
feels its way across us.

Trembling, it spills
unexplained release.

Maurice Lindsay (b. 1918)

CONTINENT O VENUS

She lies ablow my body's lust and love,
A country dearly-kent, and yet sae fremd
That she's at aince thon Tir-nan-Og I've dreamed,
The airt I've lived in, whaur I mean to live,
And mair, much mair, a mixter-maxter warld
Whaur fact and dream are taigled up and snorled.

I ken ilk bay o aa her body's strand,
Yet ken them new ilk time I come to shore,
For she's the uncharted sea whaur I maun fare
To find anither undiscovered land,
To find it fremd, and yet to find it dear,
To seek it aye, and aye be bydan there.

Alexander Scott (b. 1920)

THE SALMON-LEAP

Salmon, clean-run from new seas,
Blue-black and black-spotted, locking in an eddy
Prior to making his curve of a fish-leap:
Now rose-gill rising, ready
To hoop a steady
Bend above floodgate.
With his short taper tail's rapid hiss
The sock-eye enters. Water closes on fish.

Lover, newly arrived in fresh sight
As silverskin of atlantic littoral, descend midair
To keep my eyes under strike; plunging through,
Here salmon-leap, there
Dive, there
My regard is water smooring over the mark of you.
Implant upon my gaze headlong your lineaments;
Like sphincter muscle, depths close around them and clench.

Valerie Gillies (b. 1948)

6

Eros Exploited

THE TUA MARRIIT WEMEN AND THE WEDO

Apon the Midsummer evin, mirriest of nichtis,
I muvit furth allane, neir as midnicht wes past,
Besyd ane gudlie grein garth, full of gay flouris,
Hegeit, of ane huge hicht, with hawthorne treis;
Quhairon ane bird, on ane bransche, so birst out hir notis
That never ane blythfullar bird was on the beuche harde:
Quhat throw the sugarat sound of hir sang glaid,
And throw the savour sanative of the sueit flouris,
I drew in derne to the dyk to dirkin efter mirthis;
The dew donkit the daill and dynnit the feulis.

   I hard, under ane holyn hevinlie grein hewit,
Ane hie speiche, at my hand, with hautand wourdis;
With that in haist to the hege so hard I inthrang
That I was heildit with hawthorne and with heynd leveis:
Throw pykis of the plet thorne I presandlie luikit,
Gif one persoun wald approche within that plesand garding.

   I saw thre gay ladeis sit in ane grene arbeir,
All grathit in to garlandis of fresche gudlie flouris;
So glitterit as the gold wer thair glorius gilt tressis,
Quhill all the gressis did gleme of the glaid hewis;
Kemmit was thair cleir hair, and curiouslie sched
Attour thair schulderis doun schyre, schyning full bricht;
With curches, cassin thair abone, of kirsp cleir and thin:
Thair mantillis grein war as the gress that grew in May sessoun,
Fetrit with thair quhyt fingaris about thair fair sydis:
Off ferliful fyne favour war thair faceis meik,
All full of flurist fairheid, as flouris in June;
Quhyt, seimlie, and soft, as the sweit lillies
New upspred upon spray, as new spynist rose;
Arrayit ryallie about with mony rich vardour,

That nature full nobillie annamalit with flouris
Off alkin hewis under hevin, that ony heynd knew,
Fragrant, all full of fresche odour fynest of smell.
Ane cumlie tabil coverit wes befoir tha cleir ladeis,
With ryalle cowpis apon rawis full of ryche wynis.
And of thir fair wlonkes, tua weddit war with lordis,
Ane wes ane wedow, I wis, wantoun of laitis.
And, as thai talk at the tabill of many taill sindry,
Thay wauchtit at the wicht wyne and waris out wourdis;
And syne thai spak more spedelie, and sparit no matiris.

    Bewrie, said the Wedo, ye woddit wemen ying,
Quhat mirth ye fand in maryage, sen ye war menis wyffis;
Reveill gif ye rewit that rakles conditioun,
Or gif that ever ye luffit leyd upone lyf mair
Nor thame that ye your fayth hes festinit for ever;
Or gif ye think, had ye chois, that ye wald cheis better.
Think ye it nocht ane blist band that bindis so fast,
That none undo it a deill may bot the deith ane?

    Than spak ane lusty belyf with lustie effeiris:
It, that ye call the blist band that bindis so fast,
Is bair of blis, and bailfull, and greit barrat wirkis.
Ye speir, had I fre chois, gif I wald cheis better?
Chenyeis ay ar to eschew; and changeis ar sueit:
Sic cursit chance till eschew, had I my chois anis,
Out of the chenyeis of ane churle I chaip suld for evir.
God gif matrimony were made to mell for ane yeir!
It war bot merrens to be mair, bot gif our myndis pleisit:
It is agane the law of luf, of kynd, and of nature,
Togiddir hairtis to strene, that stryveis with uther:
Birdis hes ane better law na bernis be meikill,
That ilk yeir, with new joy, joyis ane maik,
And fangis thame ane fresche feyr, unfulyeit, and constant,
And lattis thair fulyeit feiris flie quhair thai pleis.
Cryst gif sic ane consuetude war in this kith haldin!
Than weill war us wemen that evir we war fre;
We suld have feiris as fresche to fang quhen us likit,
And gif all larbaris thair leveis, quhen thai lak curage.
My self suld be full semlie in silkis arrayit,
Gymp, jolie, and gent, richt joyus, and gentill.
I suld at fairis be found new faceis to se;
At playis, and at preichingis, and pilgrimages greit,
To schaw my renone, royaly, quhair preis was of folk,

To manifest my makdome to multitude of pepill,
And blaw my bewtie on breid, quhair bernis war mony;
That I micht cheis, and be chosin, and change quhen me lykit.
Than suld I waill ane full weill, our all the wyd realme,
That suld my womanheid weild the lang winter nicht;
And when I gottin had ane grome, ganest of uther,
Yaip, and ying, in the yok ane yeir for to draw;
Fra I had preveit his pitht the first plesand moneth,
Than suld I cast me to keik in kirk, and in markat,
And all the cuntre about, kyngis court, and uther,
Quhair I ane galland micht get aganis the nixt yeir,
For to perfurneis furth the werk quhen failyeit the tother;
A forky fure, ay furthwart, and forsy in draucht,
Nother febill, nor fant, nor fulyeit in labour,
But als fresche of his forme as flouris in May;
For all the fruit suld I fang, thocht he the flour burgeoun.

I have ane wallidrag, ane worme, ane auld wobat carle,
A waistit wolroun, na worth bot wourdis to clatter;
Ane bumbart, ane drone bee, ane bag full of flewme,
Ane skabbit skarth, ane scorpioun, ane scutarde behind;
To see him scart his awin skyn grit scunner I think.
Quhen kissis me that carybald, than kyndillis all my sorow;
As birs of ane brym bair, his berd is als stif,
Bot soft and soupill as the silk is his sary lume;
He may weill to the syn assent, bot sakles is his deidis.
With goreis his tua grym ene ar gladderrit all about,
And gorgeit lyk twa gutaris that war with glar stoppit;
Bot quhen that glowrand gaist grippis me about,
Than think I hiddowus Mahowne hes me in armes;
Thair ma na sanyne me save fra that auld Sathane;
For, thocht I croce me all cleine, fra the croun doun,
He wil my corse all beclip, and clap me to his breist.
Quhen schaiffyne is that ald schalk with a scharp rasour,
He schowis one me his schevill mouth and schedis my lippis,
And with his hard hurcheone skyn sa heklis he my chekis,
That as a glemand gleyd glowis my chaftis;
I schrenk for the scharp stound, bot schout dar I nought,
For schore of that auld schrew, schame him betide!
The luf blenkis of that bogill, fra his blerde ene,
As Belzebub had on me blent, abasit my spreit;
And quhen the smy one me smyrkis with his smake smolet,
He fepillis like a farcy aver that flyrit one a gillot.
    Quhen that the sound of his saw sinkis in my eris,

Than ay renewis my noy, or he be neir cumand:
Quhen I heir nemmyt his name, than mak I nyne crocis,
To keip me fra the cummerans of that carll mangit,
That full of eldnyng is and anger and all evill thewis.
I dar nought luke to my luf for that lene gib,
He is sa full of jelusy and engyne fals,
Ever ymagynyng in mynd materis of evill,
Compasand and castand casis a thousand
How he sall tak me, with a trawe, at trist of ane othir:
I dar nought keik to the knaip that the cop fillis,
For eldnyng of that ald schrew that ever one evill thynkis;
For he is waistit and worne fra Venus werkis,
And may nought beit worth a bene in bed of my mystirs.
He trowis that young folk I yerne, yeild for he gane is,
Bot I may yuke all this yer, or his yerd help.

      Ay quhen that caribald carll wald clyme one my wambe,
Than am I dangerus and daine and dour of my will;
Yit leit I never that larbar my leggis ga betueene,
To fyle my flesche, na fumyll me, without a fee gret;
And thoght his pene purly me payis in bed,
His purse pays richely in recompense efter:
For, or he clym on my corse, that caribald forlane,
I have conditioun of a curche of kersp allther fynest,
A goun of engranyt claith, right gaily furrit,
A ring with a ryall stane, or other riche jowell,
Or rest of his rousty raid, thoght he were rede wod:
For all the buddis of Johne Blunt, quhen he abone clymis,
Me think the baid deir aboucht, sa bawch ar his werkis;
And thus I sell him solace, thoght I it sour think:
Fra sic a syre, God yow saif, my sueit sisteris deir!

      Quhen that the semely had said her sentence to end,
Than all thai leuch apon loft with latis full mery,
And raucht the cop round about full of riche wynis,
And ralyeit lang, or thai wald rest, with ryatus speche.

      The wedo to the tothir wlonk warpit ther wordis:
Now, fair sister, fallis yow but fenyeing to tell,
Sen man ferst with matrimony yow menskit in kirk,
How haif ye farne be your faith? confese us the treuth:
That band of blise, or to ban, quhilk yow best thinkis?
Or how ye like lif to leid in to leill spousage?
And syne my self ye exeme one the samyn wise,
And I sall say furth the south, dissymyland no word.

The plesand said, I protest, the treuth gif I schaw,
That of your toungis ye be traist. The tothir twa grantit;
With that sprang up hir spreit be a span hechar.
To speik, quoth scho, I sall nought spar; ther is no spy neir:
I sall a ragment reveil fra rute of my hert,
A roust that is sa rankild quhill risis my stomok;
Now sall the byle all out brist, that beild has so lang;
For it to beir one my brist wes berdin our hevy:
I sall the venome devoid with a vent large,
And me assuage of the swalme, that suellit wes gret.

My husband wes a hur maister, the hugeast in erd,
Tharfor I hait him with my hert, sa help me our Lord!
He is a young man ryght yaip, bot nought in youth flouris,
For he is fadit full far and feblit of strenth:
He wes as flurising fresche within this few yeris,
Bot he is falyeid full far and fulyeid in labour;
He has bene lychour so lang quhill lost is his natur,
His lume is waxit larbar, and lyis in to swonne:
Wes never sugeorne werse na one that snaill tyrit,
For efter vii oulkis rest, it will nought rap anys;
He has bene waistit apone wemen, or he me wif chesit,
And in adultre, in my tyme, I haif him tane oft:
And yit he is als brankand with bonet one syde,
And blenkand to the brichtest that in the burgh duellis,
Alse curtly of his clething and kemmyng of his hair,
As he that is mare valyeand in Venus chalmer;
He semys to be sumthing worth, that syphyr in bour,
He lukis as he wald luffit be, thocht he be litill of valour;
He dois as dotit dog that damys on al bussis,
And liftis his leg apone loft, thoght he nought list pische;
He has a luke without lust and lif without curage;
He has a forme without force and fessoun but vertu,
And fair wordis but effect, all fruster of dedis;
He is for ladyis in luf a right lusty schadow,
Bot in to derne, at the deid, he salbe drup fundin;
He ralis, and makis repet with ryatus wordis,
Ay rusing him of his radis and rageing in chalmer;
Bot God wait quhat I think quhen he so thra spekis,
And how it settis him so syde to sege of sic materis.
Bot gif him self, of sum evin, myght ane say amang thaim,
Bot he nought ane is, bot nane of naturis possessoris.

Scho that has ane auld man nought all is begylit;
He is at Venus werkis na war na he semys:
I wend I josit a gem, and I haif geit gottin;

He had the glemyng of gold, and wes bot glase fundin.
Thought men be ferse, wele I fynd, fra falye ther curage,
Thar is bot eldnyng or anger ther hertis within.
Ye speik of berdis one bewch: of blise may thai sing,
That, one Sanct Valentynis day, ar vacandis ilk yer;
Hed I that plesand prevelege to part quhen me likit,
To change, and ay to cheise agane, than, chastite, adew!
Than suld I haif a fresch feir to fang in myn armes:
To hald a freke, quhill he faynt, may foly be calit.

   Apone sic materis I mus, at mydnyght, full oft,
And murnys so in my mynd I murdris my selfin;
Than ly I walkand for wa, and walteris about,
Wariand oft my wekit kyn, that me away cast
To sic a craudoune but curage, that knyt my cler bewte,
And ther so mony kene knyghtis this kenrik within:
Than think I on a semelyar, the suth for to tell,
Na is our syre be sic sevin; with that I sych oft:
Than he ful tenderly dois turne to me his tume person,
And with a yoldin yerd dois yolk me in armys,
And sais, "My soverane sueit thing, quhy sleip ye no betir?
Me think ther haldis yow a hete, as ye sum harme alyt."
Quoth I, "My hony, hald abak, and handill me nought sair;
A hache is happinit hastely at my hert rut."
With that I seme for to swoune, thought I na swerf tak;
And thus beswik I that swane with my sueit wordis:
I cast on him a crabit e, quhen cleir day is cummyn,
And lettis it is a luf blenk, quhen he about glemys,
I turne it in a tender luke, that I in tene warit,
And him behaldis hamely with hertly smyling.

   I wald a tender peronall, that myght na put thole,
That hatit men with hard geir for hurting of flesch,
Had my gud man to hir gest; for I dar God suer,
Scho suld not stert for his straik a stray breid of erd.
And syne, I wald that ilk band, that ye so blist call,
Had bund him so to that bryght, quhill his bak werkit;
And I wer in a beid broght with berne that me likit,
I trow that bird of my blis suld a bourd want.

   Onone, quhen this amyable had endit hir speche,
Loudly lauchand the laif allowit hir mekle:
Thir gay Wiffis maid game amang the grene leiffis;
Thai drank and did away dule under derne bewis;
Thai swapit of the sueit wyne, thai swanquhit of hewis,
Bot all the pertlyar in plane thai put out ther vocis.

Than said the Weido, I wis ther is no way othir;
Now tydis me for to talk; my taill it is nixt:
God my spreit now inspir and my speche quykkin,
And send me sentence to say, substantious and noble;
Sa that my preching may pers your perverst hertis,
And make yow mekar to men in maneris and conditiounis.

I schaw yow, sisteris in schrift, I wes a schrew evir,
Bot I wes schene in my schrowd, and schew me innocent;
And thought I dour wes, and dane, dispitous, and bald,
I wes dissymblit suttelly in a sanctis liknes:
I semyt sober, and sueit, and sempill without fraud,
Bot I couth sexty dissaif that suttillar wer haldin.

Unto my lesson ye lyth, and leir at me wit,
Gif you nought list be forleit with losingeris untrew:
Be constant in your governance, and counterfeit gud maneris,
Thought ye be kene, inconstant, and cruell of mynd;
Thought ye as tygris be terne, be tretable in luf,
And be as turtoris in your talk, thought ye haif talis brukill;
Be dragonis baith and dowis ay in double forme,
And quhen it nedis yow, onone, note baith ther strenthis;
Be amyable with humble face, as angellis apperand,
And with a terrebill tail be stangand as edderis;
Be of your luke like innocentis, thoght ye haif evill myndis;
Be courtly ay in clething and costly arrayit,
That hurtis yow nought worth a hen; yowr husband pays for all.

Twa husbandis haif I had, thai held me baith deir,
Thought I dispytit thaim agane, thai spyit it na thing.
Ane wes ane hair hogeart, that hostit out flewme;
I hatit him like a hund, thought I it hid preve:
With kissing and with clapping I gert the carll fone;
Weil couth I claw his cruke bak, and kemm his cowit noddill,
And with a bukky in my cheik bo on him behind,
And with a bek gang about and bler his ald e,
And with a kynd contynance kys his crynd chekis;
In to my mynd makand mokis at that mad fader,
Trowand me with trew lufe to treit him so fair.
This cought I do without dule and na dises tak,
Bot ay be mery in my mynd and myrth full of cher.

I had a lufsummar leid my lust for to slokyn,
That couth be secrete and sure and ay saif my honour,
And sew bot at certayne tymes and in sicir placis;
Ay when the ald did me anger, with akword wordis,
Apon the galland for to goif it gladit me agane.
I had sic wit that for wo weipit I litill,

Bot leit the sueit ay the sour to gud sesone bring.
Quhen that the chuf wald me chid, with girnand chaftis,
I wald him chuk, cheik, and chyn, and cheris him so mekill,
That his cheif chymys I had chevist to my sone,
Suppos the churll wes gane chaist, or the child wes gottin:
As wis woman ay I wrought and not as wod fule,
For mar with wylis I wan na wichtnes of handis.

    Syne maryit I a marchand, myghti of gudis:
He was a man of myd eld and of mene statur;
Bot we na fallowis wer in frendschip or blud,
In fredome, na furth bering, na fairnes of persoune,
Quhilk ay the fule did foryhet, for febilnes of knawlege,
Bot I sa oft thoght him on, quhill angrit his hert,
And quhilum I put furth my voce and Pedder him callit:
I wald ryght tuichandly talk be I wes tuyse maryit,
For endit wes my innocence with my ald husband:
I wes apperand to be pert within perfit eild;
Sa sais the curat of our kirk, that knew me full ying:
He is our famous to be fals, that fair worthy prelot;
I salbe laith to lat him le, quhill I may luke furth.
I gert the buthman obey, ther wes no bute ellis;
He maid me ryght hie reverens, fra he my rycht knew:
For, thocht I say it my self, the severance wes mekle
Betuix his bastard blude and my birth noble.
That page wes never of sic price for to presome anys
Unto my persone to be peir, had pete nought grantit.
Bot mercy in to womanheid is a mekle vertu,
For never bot in a gentill hert is generit ony ruth.
I held ay grene in to his mynd that I of grace tuk him,
And for he couth ken him self I curtasly him lerit:
He durst not sit anys my summondis, for, or the secund charge,
He wes ay redy for to ryn, so rad he wes for blame.
Bot ay my will wes the war of womanly natur;
The mair he loutit for my luf, the les of him I rakit;
And eik, this is a ferly thing, or I him faith gaif,
I had sic favour to that freke, and feid syne for ever:
    Quhen I the cure had all clene and him ourcummyn haill,
I crew abone that craudone, as cok that wer victour;
Quhen I him saw subject and sett at myn bydding,
Than I him lichtlyit as a lowne and lathit his maneris.
Than woxe I sa unmerciable to martir him I thought,
For as a best I broddit him to all boyis laubour:
I wald haif ridden him to Rome with raip in his heid,

Wer not ruffill of my renoune and rumour of pepill.
And yit hatrent I hid within my hert all;
Bot quhilis it hepit so huge, quhill it behud out:
Yit tuk I nevir the wosp clene out of my wyde throte,
Quhill I oucht wantit of my will or quhat I wald desir.
Bot quhen I severit had that syre of substance in erd,
And gottin his biggingis to my barne, and hie burrow landis,
Than with a stew stert out the stoppell of my hals,
That he all stunyst throu the stound, as of a stele wappin.
Than wald I, efter lang, first sa fane haif bene wrokin,
That I to flyte wes als fers as a fell dragoun.
I had for flattering of that fule fenyeit so lang,
Mi evidentis of heritagis or thai wer all selit,
My breist, that wes gret beild, bowdyn wes sa huge,
That neir my baret out brist or the band makin.
Bot quhen my billis and my bauchles wes all braid selit,
I wald na langar beir on bridill, bot braid up my heid;
Thar myght na molet mak me moy, na hald my mouth in:
I gert the renyeis rak and rif into sondir;
I maid that wif carll to werk all womenis werkis,
And laid all manly materis and mensk in this eird.
Than said I to my cumaris in counsall about,
"Se how I cabeld yone cout with a kene brydill!
The cappill, that the crelis kest in the caf mydding,
Sa curtasly the cart drawis, and kennis na plungeing,
He is nought skeich, na yit sker, na scippis nought one syd:"
And thus the scorne and the scaith scapit he nothir.
    He wes no glaidsum gest for a gay lady,
Tharfor I gat him a game that ganyt him bettir;
He wes a gret goldit man and of gudis riche;
I leit him be my lumbart to lous me all misteris,
And he wes fane for to fang fra me that fair office,
And thoght my favoris to fynd through his feill giftis.
He grathit me in a gay silk and gudly arrayis,
In gownis of engranyt claith and gret goldin chenyeis,
In ringis ryally set with riche ruby stonis,
Quhill hely raise my renoune amang the rude peple.
Bot I full craftely did keip thai courtly wedis,
Quhill eftir dede of that drupe, that dotht nought in chalmir:
Thought he of all my clathis maid cost and expense,
Ane othir sall the worschip haif, that weildis me eftir;
And thoght I likit him bot litill, yit for luf of otheris,
I wald me prunya plesandly in precius wedis,
That luffaris myght apone me luke and ying lusty gallandis,

That I held more in daynte and derer be ful mekill
Ne him that dressit me so dink: full dotit wes his heyd.
Quhen he wes heryit out of hand to hie up my honoris,
And payntit me as pako, proudest of fedderis,
I him miskennyt, be Crist, and cukkald him maid;
I him forleit as a lad and lathlyit him mekle:
I thoght my self a papingay and him a plukit herle;
All thus enforsit he his fa and fortifyit in strenth,
And maid a stalwart staff to strik him selfe doune.

   Bot of ane bowrd in to bed I sall yow breif yit:
Quhen ha ane hail year was hanyt, and him behuffit rage,
And I wes laith to be loppin with sic a lob avoir,
Alse lang as he wes on loft, I lukit on him never,
Na leit never enter in my thoght that he my thing persit,
Bot ay in mynd ane other man ymagynit that I haid;
Or ellis had I never mery bene at that myrthles raid.
Quhen I that grome geldit had of gudis and of natur,
Me thought him gracelese one to goif, sa me God help:
Quhen he had warit all one me his welth and his substance,
Me thoght his wit was all went away with the laif;
And so I did him despise, I spittit quhen I saw
That super spendit evill spreit, spulyeit of all vertu.
For, weill ye wait, wiffis, that he that wantis riches
And valyeandnes in Venus play, is ful vile haldin:
Full fruster is his fresch array and fairnes of persoune,
All is bot frutlese his effeir and falyeis at the upwith.

   I buskit up my barnis like baronis sonnis,
And maid bot fulis of the fry of his first wif.
I banyst fra my boundis his brethir ilkane;
His frendis as my fais I held at feid evir;
Be this, ye belief may, I luffit nought him self,
For never I likit a leid that langit till his blude:
And yit thir wisemen, thai wait that all wiffis evill
Ar kend with ther conditionis and knawin with the samin.

   Deid is now that dyvour and dollin in erd:
With him deit all my dule and my drery thoghtis;
Now done is my dolly ñyght, my day is upsprungin,
Adew dolour, adew! my daynte now begynis:
Now am I a wedow, I wise and weill am at ese;
I weip as I were woful, but wel is me for ever;
I busk as I wer bailfull, bot blith is my hert;
My mouth it makis murnyng, and my mynd lauchis;
My clokis thai ar caerfull in colour of sabill,
Bot courtly and ryght curyus my corse is ther undir:

I drup with a ded luke in my dule habit,
As with manis daill [I] had done for dayis of my lif.
    Quhen that I go to the kirk, cled in cair weid,
As foxe in a lambis fleise fenye I my cheir;
Than lay I furght my bright buke one breid one my kne,
With mony lusty letter ellummynit with gold;
And drawis my clok forthwart our my face quhit,
That I may spy, unaspyit, a space me beside:
Full oft I blenk by my buke, and blynis of devotioun,
To see quhat berne is best brand or bredest in schulderis,
Or forgeit is maist forcely to furnyse a bancat
In Venus chalmer, valyeandly, withoutin vane ruse:
And, as the new mone all pale, oppressit with change,
Kythis quhilis her cleir face through cluddis of sable,
So keik I through my clokis, and castis kynd lukis
To knychtis, and to cleirkis, and cortly personis.
    Quhen frendis of my husbandis behaldis me one fer,
I haif a watter spunge for wa, within my wyde clokis,
Than wring I it full wylely and wetis my chekis,
With that watteris myn ene and welteris doune teris.
Than say thai all, that sittis about, "Se ye nought, allace!
Yone lustlese led so lely scho luffit hir husband:
Yone is a pete to enprent in a princis hert,
That sic a perle of plesance suld yone pane dre!"
I sane me as I war ane sanct, and semys ane angell;
At langage of lichory I leit as I war crabit:
I sich, without sair hert or seiknes in body;
According to my sable weid I mon haif sad maneris,
Or thai will se all the suth; for certis, we wemen
We set us all fra the syght to syle men of treuth:
We dule for na evill deid, sa it be derne haldin.
    Wise wemen has wayis and wonderfull gydingis
With gret engyne to bejaip ther jolyus husbandis;
And quyetly, with sic craft, convoyis our materis
That, under Crist, no creatur kennis of our doingis.
Bot folk a cury may miscuke, that knawledge wantis,
And has na colouris for to cover thair awne kindly fautis;
As dois thir damysellis, for derne dotit lufe,
That dogonis haldis in dainte and delis with thaim so lang,
Quhill all the cuntre knaw ther kyndnes and faith:
Faith has a fair name, bot falsheid faris bettir:
Fy one hir that can nought feyne her fame for to saif!
Yit am I wise in sic werk and wes all my tyme;
Thoght I want wit in warldlynes, I wylis haif in luf,

As ony happy woman has that is of hie blude:
Hutit be the halok las a hunder yeir of eild!
    I have ane secrete servand, rycht sobir of his toung,
That me supportis of sic nedis, quhen I a syne mak:
Thoght he be sympill to the sicht, he has a tong sickir;
Full mony semelyar sege wer service dois mak:
Thought I haif cair, under cloke, the cleir day quhill nyght,
Yit haif I solace, under serk, quhill the sone ryse.
    Yit am I haldin a haly wif our all the haill schyre,
I am sa peteouse to the pur, quhen ther is personis mony.
In passing of pilgrymage I pride me full mekle,
Mair for the prese of peple na ony perdoun wynyng.
    Bot yit me think the best bourd, quhen baronis and knychtis,
And othir bachilleris, blith blumyng in youth,
And all my luffaris lele, my lugeing persewis,
And fyllis me wyne wantonly with weilfair and joy:
Sum rownis; and sum ralyeis: and sum redis ballatis;
Sum raiffis furght rudly with riatus speche;
Sum plenis, and sum prayis; sum prasis mi bewte,
Sum kissis me; sum clappis me; sum kyndnes me proferis;
Sum kerffis to me curtasli; sum me the cop giffis;
Sum stalwardly steppis ben, with a stout curage,
And a stif standand thing staiffis in my neiff;
And mony blenkis ben our, that but full fer sittis,
That mai, for the thik thrang, nought thrif as thai wald.
Bot, with my fair calling, I comfort thaim all:
For he that sittis me nixt, I nip on his finger;
I serf him on the tothir syde on the samin fasson;
And he that behind me sittis, I hard on him lene;
And him befor, with my fut fast on his I stramp;
And to the bernis far but sueit blenkis I cast:
To every man in speciall speke I sum wordis
So wisly and so womanly, quhill warmys ther hertis.
    Thar is no liffand leid so law of degre
That sall me luf unluffit, I am so loik hertit;
And gif his lust so be lent into my lyre quhit,
That he be lost or with me lig, his lif sall nocht danger.
I am so mercifull in mynd, and menys all wichtis,
My sely saull salbe saif, quhen Sabot all jugis.
Ladyis leir thir lessonis and be no lassis fundin:
This is the legeand of my lif, thought Latyne it be nane.

    Quhen endit had her ornat speche, this eloquent wedow,
Lowd thai lewch all the laif, and loffit hir mekle,

And said thai suld exampill tak of her soverane teaching,
And wirk efter hir wordis, that woman wes so prudent.
Than culit thai thair mouthis with confortable drinkis,
And carpit full cummerlik with cop going round.

Thus draif thai our that deir nyght with danceis full noble,
Quhill that the day did up daw, and dew donkit flouris;
The morow myld wes and meik, the mavis did sing,
And all remuffit the myst, and the meid smellit;
Silver schouris doune schuke as the schene cristall,
And berdis schoutit in schaw with thair schill notis;
The goldin glitterand gleme so gladit ther hertis;
Thai maid a glorious gle amang the grene bewis.
The soft sowch of the swyr and soune of the stremys,
The sueit savour of the sward and singing of foulis,
Myght confort ony creatur of the kyn of Adam,
And kindill agane his curage, thocht it wer cald sloknyt.
Than rais thir ryall roisis, in ther riche wedis,
And rakit hame to ther rest through the rise blumys;
And I all prevely past to a plesand arber,
And with my pen did report thair pastance most mery.

Ye auditoris most honorable, that eris has gevin
Oneto this uncouth aventur, quhilk airly me happinnit:
Of thir thre wantoun wiffis, that I haif writtin heir,
Quhilk wald ye waill to your wif, gif ye suld wed one?

William Dunbar (c. 1465-c. 1513)

LUCKY SPENCE'S LAST ADVICE*

Thee times the carline grain'd and rifted,
Then frae the cod her pow she lifted,
In bawdy policy well gifted,
   When she now faun,
That Death na langer wad be shifted,
   She thus began:

My loving lasses, I maun leave ye,
But dinna wi' ye'r greeting grieve me,
Nor wi' your draunts and droning deave me,
   But bring's a gill;
For faith, my bairns, ye may believe me,
   'Tis 'gainst my will.

O black-ey'd Bess and mim-mou'd Meg,
O'er good to work or yet to beg;
Lay sunkots up for a sair leg,
                    For whan ye fail,
Ye'r face will not be worth a feg,
                    Nor yet y'er tail.

When e'er ye meet a fool that's fow,
That ye're a maiden gar him trow,
Seem nice, but stick to him like glew;
                    And whan set down,
Drive at the jango till he spew,
                    Syne he'll sleep soun.

Whan he's asleep, then dive and catch
His ready cash, his rings or watch;
And gin he likes to light his match
                    At your spunk-box,
Ne'er stand to let the fumbling wretch
                    E'en take the pox.

Cleek a' ye can be hook or crook;
Ryp ilky poutch frae nook to nook;
Be sure to truff his pocket-book,
                    Saxty pounds Scots
Is nae deaf nits: In little bouk
                    Lie great bank-notes.

To get a mends of whinging fools,
That's frighted for repenting-stools,
Wha often, whan their metal cools,
                    Turn sweer to pay,
Gar the kirk-boxie hale the dools
                    Anither day.

But dawt Red Coats, and let them scoup,
Free for the fou of cutty stoup;
To gee them up, ye need na hope
                    E'er to do well:
They'll rive ye'r brats and kick your doup,
                    And play the Deel.

There's ae sair cross attends the craft,
That curst Correction-house, where aft

Vild Hangy's taz ye're riggings saft
              Makes black and blae,
Enough to pit a body daft;
              But what'll ye say.

Nane gathers gear withouten care,
Ilk pleasure has of pain a skare;
Suppose then they should tirl ye bare,
              And gar ye fike,
E'en learn to thole; 'tis very fair
              Ye're nibour like.

Forby, my looves, count upo' losses,
Ye're milk-white teeth and cheeks like roses,
Whan jet-black hair and brigs of noses
              Faw down wi' dads
To keep your hearts up 'neath sic crosses,
              Set up for bawds.

Wi' well-crish'd loofs I hae been canty,
Whan e'er the lads wad fain ha'e faun t'ye;
To try the auld game Taunty Raunty,
              Like coofers keen,
They took advice of me your aunty,
              If ye were clean.

Then up I took my siller ca'
And whistl'd ben whiles ane, whiles twa;
Roun'd in his lug, that there was a
              Poor country Kate,
As halesom as the well of Spaw,
              But unka blate.

Sae whan e'er company came in,
And were upo' a merry pin,
I slade away wi' little din
              And muckle mense,
Left conscience judge, it was a' ane
              To Lucky Spence.

My bennison come on good doers,
Who spend their cash on bawds and whores;
May they ne'er want the wale of cures

                      For a sair snout:
              Foul fa' the quacks wha that fire smoors,
                              And puts nae out.

              My malison light ilka day
              On them that drink, and dinna pay,
              But tak a snack and rin away;
                              May't be their hap
              Never to want a gonorrhoea,
                              Or rotten clap.

              Lass gi'e us in anither gill,
              A mutchken, Jo, let's tak our fill;
              Let Death syne registrate his bill
                              Whan I want sense,
              I'll slip away with better will,
                              Quo' Lucky Spence.
                                        Allan Ramsay (1686–1758)

                          NICHT O LUST*

          I got her i the Black Bull
              (The Black Bull o Norroway)
          Gin I mynd richt, in Leith Street,
          Doun the stair at the corner forenent
          The Fun Fair and Museum o Monstrosities,
              The Tyke-faced Loun, the Cunyiars' Den
                  And siclike.

          I tine her name the nou, and cognomen for that—
          Aiblins it was Deirdre, Ariadne, Calliope,
          Gaby, Jacquette, Katerina, Sandra
              Or sunkots; exotic, I expeck.
          A week bit piece
              O' what our faithers maist unaptlie
              But romanticallie designatit "Fluff."
          My certie! Nae muckle o Fluff
              About the hures of Reekie!
          Dour as stane, the like stane
          As biggit the unconquerable citie
          Whaur they pullulate,
                              Infestan

The wynds and closes, squares
And public promenads
      —The bonnie craturies!
            —But til our winter's tale.

—Ah, she was a bonnie cou!
Saxteen, maybe sevinteen, nae mair,
Her mither in attendance, *comme il faut*
*Pour les jeunes filles bien elev*ées,
   Drinkan like a bluidie whaul tae!
Wee paps, round and ticht and fou
Like sweet Pomona in the ornager grove;
Her shanks were lang, but no owre lang, and plump,
   A lassie's shanks,
Wi the meisurance o Venus—
   Achteen inch the hoch frae heuchle-bane til knap,
   Achteen inch the cauf frae knap til cuit
As is the true perfectioun calculate
By the Auntients efter due regaird
For this and that,
             The true meisurance
   O' the Venus dei Medici,
   The Aphrodite Anadyomene
And aa the goddesses o hie antiquitie—
   Siclike were the shanks and hochs
O' Sandra the cou o the auld Black Bull.
   Her een were, naiturallie, expressionless,
Blank as chuckie-stanes, like the bits
O' blae-green gless ye find by the sea.
          —Nostalgia! Ah, sweet regrets!—
   Her blee was yon o sweet sexteen,
Her lire as white as Dian's chastitie
   In yon fyle, fousome, clortie slum.
Sound the tocsin, sound the drum!
The Haas o Balclutha ring wi revelrie!
The Prince sall dine at Hailie Rude the nicht!

   The lums o the reikan toun
   Spreid aa ablow, and round
   As far as ye could look
   The yalla squares o winnocks
   Lit ilkane by a nakit yalla sterne
   Blenkan, aff, syne on again,
   Out and in and out again,

As the thrang mercat throve,
  The haill toun at it,
Aa the lichts pip-poppan
  In and out and in again
    I' the buts and bens
      And single ends,
        The banks and braes
O' the toueran cliffs o lands,
Haill tenements, wards and burghs, counties,
  Regalities and jurisdictiouns,
    Continents and empires
    Gien ower entire
Til the joukerie-poukerie!
Hech, sirs, whatna feck o fockerie!
Shades o Knox, the hochmagandie!
  My bonie Edinburrie,
    Auld Skulduggerie!
Flat on her back sevin nichts o the week,
Earnan her breid wi her hurdies' sweit.

—And Dian's siller chastitie
Muved owre the reikan lums,
Biggan a ferlie toun o jet and ivorie
That was but blackened stane,
Whar Bothwell rade and Huntly
And fair Montrose and aa the lave
Wi silken leddies doun til the grave.
  —The hoofs strak siller on the causie!
    And I mysel in cramasie!

There Sandra sleepan, like a doe shot
I' the midnicht wuid, wee paps
Like munes, mune-aipples gaithert
  I' the Isles o Youth,
Her flung straucht limbs
 A paradisal archipelagie
Inhaudan divers bays, lagoons,
Great carses, strands and sounds,
Islands and straits, peninsulies,
  Whar traders, navigators,
  Odyssean gangrels, gubernators,
  Mutineers and maister-marineers
And aa sic outland chiels micht utilise wi ease
Cheap flouered claiths and beads,

Gauds, wire and sheenan nails
    And siclike flichtmafletherie
In fair and just excambion
For aa the ferlies o the southren seas
That chirm in thy deep-dernit creeks,
    —My Helen douce as aipple-jack
        That cack't the bed in exstasie!
Ah, belle nostalgie de la boue!

—Sandra, princess-leman o a nicht o lust,
    That girdlet the fishie seas
    Frae Leith til Honolulu,
    Maistress o the white mune Cytherean,
        Tak this bardic tribute nou!
    Immortalitie sall croun thy heid wi bays,
        Laurel and rosemarie and rue!
    You that spierit me nae questions,
        Spierit at me nocht,
            Acceptit me and took me in
            A guest o the house, nae less;
    Took aa there was to gie
        (And yon was peerie worth),
    Gied what ye didna loss—
            A bien and dernit fleeman's-firth
            And bodie's easement
            And saft encomfortin!
    O Manon! Marguerite! Camille!
        And maybe, tae, the pox—
                        Ach, weill!
                        Sydney Goodsir Smith (1915–1975)

FAT MARGET'S BALLADE*
(From the French of Villon)

If my weel-willied dame I serve an love,
Man I be held a toetak or a nyaff?
In her is every bliss your hert can muv,
An, feth, nor sword nor shield tae fend ye aff;
Fur, whin da men come, I rin furt an skaff
A pint or twa, no toed at laek a foel.
I bring dem maet ta aet an watter coel,
An if dey pey weel, tell dem: "Sae be dat!

Come ye again whin niest ye're arg tae roel,
Here i dis hoorhoose whaar we had wis at."

Bit, later on, dir herns an wallawa,
Whin Marget comes to bed ithoot a plack:
I canna lyeuk at her, her neck I'd traa;
Her cotts, her slug, her buckled belt I tak
An swear A'll roup da lot ta get my wack.
Wi haands on hips, dis Antichrist roars oot
An swears by Jesus on da Cross at cloot
Or plag I sanna. Dan I nam a slat
An wraet a bloedy answer on her snoot,
Here i dis hoorhoose whaar we had wis at.

Dan we mak pace; she slips a monstrous fart
(Shoe's ey as blaan-up as a bloed-swalled bug).
Laachin, shoe lays her hand on me, an: "Start!
Vite! Vite!" she says, an gies my prick a nug . . .
Syne, baith daid drunk, we sleep as soon's a clug
Bit, whin shoe waakens an still feels da yuck,
Shoe climms in tap, fur faer her seed wants muck;
I gron below, as ony plank pressed flat.
Wi sic bed-wark, shoe's laid me fair in bruck,
Here i dis hoorhoose whaar we had wis at.

Snaa, hail, or blaa, I hae my bite o maet.
Sae be's A'm bitched, da bitch is still in haet.
Wha's wirt da maest? We baith gang da wan gaet.
Tane wards da tidder; da cat's as ill's da rat.
As we laek sharn, shite shaests wis shoen an late.
We skail fae honour, an hit's joest as blate,
Here i dis hoorhoose whaar we had wis at.

William J. Tait (b. 1918)

SOHO*

dutch straps mr universe jock caps 1001 nights genuine rechy
fully tested adolescence & box 5/- only velasquez
kalpa baggers naturist bargain guide original sex carpet
sutra hill transvestism before marriage more inside
kama books fanny goods family nudes free each purch
planning our own petronius durex opedia

history of the genet established insertion imported
lubricated health best of the flowers
human hygienic capital rod no obligatio
lash purgated quatrefoil masochism
unex punishment trusses george ryley scott soft yet firm
5 capital practices for men 7/6 ea
life of skin thin witchcraft variants
technique of hirschf strap psycho many lands nus
homosex encyclo erotica the set nothing like the sun
30/- psycholo oriental rubber burton leather boys
author of amazing years of diaphragm
desire and pursuit of the marquis de sutra au cinema
health & wrestling jours de sodom unbeatable
william burroughs shakespeare complete dead fingers
cacti and succulent flagellation havelock and after
handy pathia sexu ellis ready reckoner
rhythm method works quentin per crisp cent
ten tom jones tablets belt recommended
our lady of the litesome
wuthering heights full protection
boxing & vaseline fully illustrated hosiery
ABZ of unrepeatable tropic of enemas
who's afraid of virginia goldfinger
dr no guide to london heller orgies book of the f
20,000 leagues under angus wilson yoga fetishism agency
traps omar khayyam a week's supply for pocket torture photogr
chinese medical cooking in 80 days lo duca come in and browse
trial of oscar mickey fleming birth-cont catch-22 hyde miller
no mean city of night prophylactic burgess anomalies
johnson & johnson john o' hara john calder judo spillane karate
transparent KY water soluble cookbook
an unhurried view of impotence rock plants and alpines
oxford book of english prostitution
youth requisites sterilized plain white
slightly washable shop soiled down the ages

    But to wash London
                would take a sea.
    To want to wash it
                history.

    Now bury this poem in one of the vaults
    of our civilisation, and let the Venusian
    computers come down, and searching for life

crack our ghastly code.
Bury it, bury it! Who cares?
   We shall never know.
We've buried worse, with mouths to feed.
   And so . . . And so . . . And so . . .
Polish the window, bury the poem, and go.

Edwin Morgan (b. 1920)

THE FAN*

I make it seem and seem you see it. That's my art.
The art despises body-stockings, needs
its dark stage, pearly spotlight on the plumes,
honkytonk strains, it needs
the programmes waved as fans in the hot stalls
to be stilled. Let each eye strain.
I ruffle and quiver,
my ostrich feathers breathe
with the breasts beneath them,
I slide and flash, subside,
cross and re-cross,
wisps of plume drift off,
swirl in the tunnel of light.
I've got my dancer in my arms.
Out there, you'll never come so close,
get nipples and belly in a drean
and only as sweet as a dream thrown
on cigarette smoke and waves of heat and sound
like a screen. I am the screen
of what standing still would cheapen,
a beauty that moves and is never seen.

Edwin Morgan (b. 1920)

TO MOURN JAYNE MANSFIELD
(Decapitated in a car crash, June 1967)

I
SAIR SONNET
Cauld is thon corp that fleered sae muckle heat,
Thae Bablyon breists that gart the bishops ban

And aa the teeny titties grain and greet
That siccan sichts should gawp the ee o man.

Still are the hurdies steered sic houghmagandie,
The hips saw swack, their ilka step a swee,
That graybeards maun hae risen hauflin-randie
To merk them move and move the yirth agee.

Faan is thon powe that crouned her fairheid's flouer,
Hackit awa as gin by the heidsman's aix—
Our lust the blade has killed thon bonnie hure,
Puir quine! that aince had reigned the Queen o Glaiks.

Owre aa the warld the standards canna stand,
Wauchied their strength as onie willow-wand.

II
HOLLYWOOD IN HADES
Jayne Mansfield, strippit mortal stark
    O' aa her orra duddies—
For thae that sail in Charon's barque
    Keep nocht aside their bodies—
Comes dandily daffan til Hades' dark,
    A sicht to connach studies.

Yet Pluto, coorse as King Farouk,
    Gies only ae bit glower—
She's naukit, ilka sonsie neuk,
    But he's seen aa afore—
And turns to tell the t'ither spook,
    "Marilyn, move outowre!"

Alexander Scott (b. 1920)

A VICTORIAN VICTIM
(W. T. Stead's *The Maiden Tribute of Modern Babylon*, published in 1885,
was featured on television in 1976.)

Unbudded breasts, frail limbs, the narrow loins
 As bare as the flinching face with haunted eyes,
This childish "daughter of joy" is mother of shame
For us her offspring, spawn of that womb's defilement,
Who see her stripped to the letch of another lens

As televised history, hissing Victorian vice,
Still uses the ancient camera's avid eye
To peer through time at the plunder of torment past,
At innocence bought for the brothel, drugged, deflowered,
Then posed in trophy, pictured as maid unmade,
Too young for love, already old in anguish,
Bare below flinching face and haunted eyes
Unbudded breasts, frail limbs, and narrow loins.

What anguish now? If any, undisclosed.
From page upon glossy page the girlies grin
To strip themselves starkers, bouncing bountiful boobs
And bending backs to hoist up cheeky haunches
And straddling the wink of thatch with widespread thighs
And petting privates, easing the public itch
With playful fingers practised in fudging joy.

Farewell, Victoria! Victim, a fond farewell!
You suffered, slave.
                    But this is our liberation.

                                        Alexander Scott (b. 1920)

7

Eros Decried/Denied

ROBENE AND MAKYNE*

Robene sat on a gud grene hill
Kepand a flok of fe;
Mirry Makyne said him till:
"Robene, thow rew on me!
I haif the luvit lowd and still
Thir yeiris two or thre;
My dule in dern bot gif thow dill,
Dowtles but dreid I de."

Robene ansuerit: "Be the Rude,
Nathing of lufe I knaw,
Bot keipis my scheip under yone [wude]—
Lo quhair thay raik on raw!
Quhat hes marrit the in thy mude,
Makyne, to me thow schaw:
Or quhat is lufe, or to be lude?
Fane wald I leir that law."

"At luvis lair gife thow will leir,
Tak thair ane ABC:
Be heynd, courtas and fair of feir,
Wyse, hardy and fre;
So that no denger do the deir,
Quhat dule in dern thow dre,
Preis the with pane at all poweir—
Be patient and previe."

Robene ansuerit hir agane:
"I wait nocht quhat is luve,
Bot I haif mervell in certane

Quhat makis the this wanrufe;
The weddir is fair and I am fane,
My scheip gois haill aboif;
And we wald play us in this plane
Thay wald us bayth reproif."

"Robene, tak tent unto my taill,
And wirk all as I reid,
And thow sall haif my hairt all haill,
Eik and my madinheid:
Sen God sendis bute for baill
And for murnyng remeid,
I dern with the bot gif I daill,
Dowtles I am bot deid."

"Makyne, tomorne this ilka tyde,
And ye will meit me heir,
Peraventure my scheip ma gang besyd
Quhill we haif liggit full neir—
Bot mawgre haif I and I byd,
Fra thay begin to steir;
Quhat lyis on hairt I will nocht hyd;
Makyn, than mak gud cheir."

"Robene, thow reivis me roif and rest—
I luve bot the allone."
"Makyne, adew; the sone gois west,
The day is neir-hand gone."
"Robene, in dule I am so drest
That lufe wil be my bone."
"Ga lufe, Makyne, quhairever thow list,
For lemman I lue none."

"Robene, I stand in sic a styll;
I sich—and that full sair."
"Makyne, I haif bene heir this quhyle;
At hame God gif I wair!"
"My huny Robene, talk ane quhill,
Gif thow will do na mair."
"Makyne, sum uthir man begyle,
For hamewart I will fair."

Robene on his wayis went
Als licht as leif of tre;

Mawkin murnit in hir intent
And trowd him nevir to se.
Robene brayd attour the bent;
Than Mawkyne cryit on hie:
"Now ma thow sing, for I am schent!
Quhat alis lufe at me?"

Mawkyne went hame withowttin faill;
Full wery eftir cowth weip:
Than Robene in a ful fair daill
Assemblit all his scheip.
Be that, sum pairte of Mawkynis aill
Outthrow his hairt cowd creip;
He fallowit fast thair till assaill,
And till hir tuke gude keip.

"Abyd, abyd, thow fair Makyne!
A word for ony thing!
For all my luve it sal be thyne,
Withowttin depairting.
All haill thy harte for till haif myne
Is all my cuvating;
My scheip tomorne quhill houris nyne
Will neid of no keiping."

"Robene, thow hes hard soung and say
In gestis and storeis auld,
The man that will nocht quhen he may
Sall haif nocht quhen he wald.
I pray to Jesu every day
Mot eik thair cairis cauld
That first preiss with the to play
Be firth, forrest or fawld."

"Makyne, the nicht is soft and dry,
The wedder is warme and fair,
And the grene woid rycht neir us by
To walk attour allquhair;
Thair ma na janglour us espy,
That is to lufe contrair;
Thairin, Makyne, bath ye and I
Unsene we ma repair."

"Robene, that warld is all away
And quyt brocht till ane end,
And nevir agane thairto perfay,
Sall it be as thow wend:
For all my pane thow maid it play,
And all in vane I spend:
As thow hes done, sa sall I say:
Murne on! I think to mend."

"Mawkyne, the howp of all my heill,
My hairt on the is sett,
And evirmair to the be leill,
Quhill I may leif but lett;
Nevir to faill—as utheris feill—
Quhat grace that evir I gett."
"Robene, with the I will nocht deill;
Adew! For thus we mett."

Malkyne went hame blyth annewche
Attour the holttis hair:
Robene murnit, and Malkyne lewche,
Scho sang, he sichit sair—
And so left him bayth wo and wrewche,
In dolour and in cair,
Kepand his hird under a huche,
Amang the holtis hair.

Robert Henryson (c. 1420–c. 1490)

REPUDIATION*

Quhen Diomeid had all his appetyte,
And mair, fulfillit of this fair ladie,
Upon ane uther he set his haill delyte,
And send to hir ane lybell of repudie
And hir excludit fra his companie.
Than desolait scho walkit up and doun,
And sum men sayis, into the court, commoun.

O fair Creisseid, the flour and A per se
Of Troy and Greece, how was thow fortunait
To change in filth all thy feminitie,
And be with fleschelie lust sa maculait,

And go amang the Greikis air and lait,
Sa gigotlike takand thy foull plesance!
I have pietie thow suld fall in sic mischance!

As custome was, the pepill far and neir
Befoir the none unto the tempill went
With sacrifice, devoit in thair maneir;
Bot still Cresseid, hevie in hir intent,
Into the kirk wald not hir self present,
For giving of the pepill ony deming
Of hir expuls fra Diomeid the king;

Bot past into ane secreit orature,
Quhair scho micht weip hir wofull desteny.
Behind hir bak scho cloisit fast the dure
And on hir kneis bair fell doun in hy;
Upon Venus and Cupide angerly
Scho cryit out, and said on this same wyse,
"Allace, that ever I maid yow sacrifice!

"Ye gave me anis ane devine responsaill
That I suld be the flour of luif in Troy;
Now am I maid ane unworthie outwaill,
And all in cair translatit is my joy.
Quha sall me gyde? Quha sall me now convoy,
Sen I fra Diomeid and nobill Troylus
Am clene excludit, as abject odious?

"O fals Cupide, is nane to wyte bot thow
And thy mother, of lufe the blind goddes!
Ye causit me alwayis understand and trow
The seid of lufe was sawin in my face,
And ay grew grene throw your supplie and grace.
Bot now, allace, that seid with froist is slane,
And I fra luiffers left, and all forlane."

Robert Henryson (c. 1420–c. 1490)

WAE WORTH MARRIAGE

In Bowdoun on Blak Monunday,
quehen all was gadderit to the play,
bayth men and women semblit thair,

I hard ane sweit ane sicht and say,
'Way worth maryage for evermair!

Madinis, ye may have grit plesance
for to do Venus observance,
thocht I inclusit be with cair
that I dar nother sing nor dance.
Wa worth maryage for evirmair!—

Quhen that I was ane madein ying,
lichtlie wald I dance and sing
and sport and play bayth lait and air.
Now dar I nocht luik to sic thing.
Way wourth maryage for evirmair!

Thus am I bundin out of blis
on to ane churle sayis I am his,
that I dar nocht luik our the stair
Scantlie to gif sir Johne ane kis.
Wa worth maryage for evirmair!

Now war I ane madin as I wes,
to mak me lady of the Bas,
and thocht that I wer never so fair,
to weddin suld I never pas.
Way worth maryage for evirmair!

Thus am I thirlit on to ane schrew
quhilk dow nothing of chalmer glew,
off bowre bourding bayth bask and bair.
God wayt gif I have caus to rew!—
Way worth maryage for evirmair!

All nicht I clatter upoin my creid,
prayand to God gif I were deid,
or ellis out of this warld I wair.
Than suld I se for sum remeid.
Way wourth maryage for evirmair!

Ye suld heir tell, and he wer gane,
that I suld be ane wantoun ane
to leir the law of luiffis layr.
In our toun lyk me suld be nane.
Way worth maryage for evirmair!

I suld put on my russet gowne,
my reid kirtill, my hois of broun,
and lat them se my yallow hair
undir my curche hingand doun.
Way wourth maryage for evirmair!

Luffaris bayth suld heir and se
I suld luif thame that wald luif me.
Thair hartis for me suld never be sair.
Bot ay unweddit suld I be.
Way wourth maryage for evirmair!"

Sir George Clapperton (c. 1505–1574)

WANTON WEMEN

Ye lusty ladyis luke
The rakles lyfe ye leid,
Hant nocht in hoile or nuke
To hurt your womanheid;
I reid, for best remeid,
Forbeir all place prophane:
Gife this be caus of feid,
I sall not said agane.

Quhat is sic luve bot lust,
A lytill for delyte,
To hant that game robust,
And beistly appetyte;
I nowdir fleische nor flyte,
To tell the trewith certaine;
Taik ye this in despyte,
I sall not said agane.

The wysest scho may sone
Sedusit be and schent;
Syne fra the deid be done,
Perchance sall soir repent;
Ouir lait is till lament
Fra belly dow not lane,
To try in tyme take tent:
I sall not said agane.

Lycht wynchis luve will fawin,
Evin lyk an spanyeollis lawchter,
To lat hir wamb be clawin
Be them list geir betawcht hir;
For conyie ye may chawcht hir,
To sched hir schankis in twane,
And nevir speir quais awcht hir:
I sall not said agane.

Thocht bruckill wemen hantis
In lust to leid thair lyvis,
And wedow men that wantis
To steill a pair of swyvis;
Bot quhair that mareit wyvis
Gois by thair husbandis bane,
That houshald nevir thryvis;
I sall not said agane.

It settis not madynis als
To latt men lowis thair laice
Nor clym about menis halss,
To clap, to kiss, nor braice,
Nor round in secreit place;
Sic treitment is a trane
To cleive thair quaver-caice:
I sall not said agane.

Fairweill with chestetie,
Fra wenchis fall to chucking,
Thair followis thingis thre
To gar thame ga in gucking,
Brasing, Graping, and Plucking;
Thir foure the suth to sane,
Enforsis thame to fucking:
I sall not said agane.

Sum luvis new cum to toun,
With jeigs to mak thame joly,
Sum luvis dance up and doun,
To meiss thair malancoly;
Sum luvis lang trollie-lolly,
And sum of frigging fane,
Lyk fillokkis full of folly:
I sall not said agane.

Sum monebrunt madynis myld,
At nonetyd of the nicht,
Are chappit up with chyld,
But coil or candill-licht;
Sua sum said maidis hes slicht
To play, and tak no pane,
Syne chift thair seid fra sicht:
I sall not said agane.

Sum thinkis na schame to clap
And kiss in opin wyiss;
Sum can-nocht keip hir gap
Fra lansing as scho lyiss;
Sum gois so gymp in gyiss,
Or scho war kissit plane,
Scho leir be japit thryiss:
I sall not said agane.

Moir gentrice is to jott
Undir ane silkin goun,
Nor ane quhyt pittecott
And reddyar ay boun;
The denkest sonnest doun,
The farest but refrane,
The gayest grittest loun:
I sall not said again.

The moir degest and grave,
The grydiar to grip it;
The nycest to ressave,
Upoun the nynnis will nip it;
The quhytliest will quhip it,
And nocht her hurdeis hane;
The less the lerger hippit:
I sall not said again.

Loe! ladeis gif this bie,
Ane gud counsale I geif yow,
To saive your honestie,
Fra sklander to releif yow;
Bot ballads ma to breif yow,
I will nocht brek my brane,
Suppois ye sowld mischeif yow;
I sall not said again.

Alexander Scott (c. 1515–c. 1583)

BLINDED LOVERS*

Ye blindit luvers luke
The rekless lyfe ye leid;
Espy the snair and huke
That haldis yow be the heid:
Thairfoir, I reid remeid,
To leife and lat it be;
For lufe hes non at feid
Bot fulis that can nocht fle.

Quhat is your lufe bot lust,
Ane littill for delyte,
Ane beistly game robust,
To reif your ressoun quyte;
Ane fowsum appetyte,
That strenth of persoun waikis;
Ane pastance unperfyte,
To smyte yow with the glaikis.

Quhair sensuall lust proceidis,
All honest lufe is pynd;
Ye may compair your deidis,
Unto ane brutall kynd;
Fra vertew be constrynd
To follow vyce, considdir
That ressoun, wit, and mynd,
Ar all ago togiddir.

The wysest woman thairout,
With wirdis may be wylit
To do the deid but dout,
That honour hes exyllit:
How mony ar begyllit,
And few I fynd that chaipis;
Thairfoir your faithis ar fylit
To frawd thay silly aipis.

Ye mak regaird for grace
Quhair nevir grace yit grew;
Ye lang to ryn the race
That ane or baith sall rew;
Ye preiss ay to persew
Thair syte and your awin sorrow;

Ye trest to find thame trew,
That nevir wes beforrow.

Ye cry on Cupeid king
And Venus quene in vane;
Ye send all manner thing
With trattillis thame to trane;
Ye preiche, ye fleich, ye frane;
Ye grane ay quhill thay grant;
Your prectikis ar profane,
Pure ladeis to supplant.

Ye schowt as ye wer schent,
Thay swoun to se yow smartit;
Ye rame as ye were rent,
And thay ar rewthfull hairtit;
Your plays ar sone pervertit,
Fra that thair belly ryss;
Thay wary yow that gart it,
And ye thame in lykwyss.

Yit thair is lesum lufe
That lawchtfully suld lest;
He is nocht to reprufe
That is with ane possest:
That band I hald it best,
And nocht to pass attour;
Bot ye can tak no rest
Quhill thay kast up all four.

Sic luvaris sendill meitis,
Bot ladeis ay forlorne is;
Quhen thay bewaill and greitis,
Sum of yow lawchis and skornis:
Your hecht, yoir aith mensworne is,
Your lippis ar lyk burd-lyme;
I hald ye want bot hornis,
As bukkis in belling time.

Ye trattill and ye tyst,
Quhill thay forget thair fame;
Ye trane thame to ane tryst,
And thair ye get thame tame:
Thay sussy nocht for schame,

Nor cast nocht quhat comes syne;
Bot quhen ye claw thair wame,
Thay tummyll our lyk swyne.

Alexander Scott (c. 1515–c. 1583)

WHOREDOM*

Near some lamp-post, wi' dowy face,
Wi' heavy een, and sour grimace,
Stands she that beauty lang had kend,
Whoredom her trade, and vice her end.
But see wharenow she wuns her bread,
By that which Nature ne'er decreed;
And sings sad music to the lugs,
'Mang burachs o' damn'd whores and rogues.
Whane'er we reputation loss,
Fair chastity's transparent gloss!
Redemption seenil kens the name
But a's black misery and shame.

Robert Fergusson (1750–1774)

FROM THE FRENCH

It chanced that Cupid on a season
By Fancy urged, resolved to wed,
But could not settle whether Reason
Or Folly should partake his bed.

What does he then?—Upon my life,
'Twas bad example for a deity,
He takes me Reason for a wife,
And Folly for his hours of gaiety.

Though thus he dealt in petty treason,
He loved them both in equal measure;
Fidelity was born of Reason,
And Folly brought to bed of Pleasure.

Sir Walter Scott (1771–1832)

THE JAUD

"O what are ye seein', ye auld wife,
   I' the bield o' the kirkyaird wa'?"
"I see a place whaur the grass is lang
   Wi' the great black nettles grawn fierce an' strang
     And a stane that is clour'd in twa."

"What way div ye glower, ye auld wife,
   Sae lang on the whumml'd stane?
Ye hae nae kin that are sleepin' there,
Yer three braw dochters are guid an' fair
    An' ilk wi' a man o' her ain!

"There's dule an' tears i' yer auld een
   Tho' little eneuch ye lack;
Yer man is kindly, as weel ye ken,
Yer fower bauld laddies are thrivin' men
    And ilk wi' a fairm at his back.

"Turn, turn yer face frae yon cauld lair
   And back tae yer plenished hame;
It's a jaud lies yont i' the nettle shaws
Whaur niver a blink o' the sunlicht fa's
    On the mools that hae smoor'd her name."

"Her hair was gowd like the gowd broom,
   Her een like the stars abune,
Sae prood an' lichtsome an' fine was she
Wi' her breist like the flowers o' the white rose tree
    When they're lyin' below the mune."

"Haud you yer havers, ye auld wife,
   Think shame o' the words ye speak,
Tho' men lay fast in her beauty's grip
She brocht the fleer tae the wumman's lip
    An' the reid tae the lassie's cheek.

"Ye've lived in honour, ye auld wife,
   But happit in shame she lies,
And them that kent her will turn awa'
When the Last Day braks tae the trumpet's ca'
    And the sauls o' the righteous rise."

"Maybe. But lave me tae bide my lane
At the fit o' the freendless queyn;
For oh! wi' envy I'm like tae dee
O' the warld she had that was no for me
And the kingdom that ne'er was mine!"

Violet Jacob (1863–1946)

IN THE ORCHARD

"I thought you loved me."

                    "No, it was only fun."

"When we stood there, closer than all?"

                              "Well, the harvest moon
Was shining and queer in your hair, and it turned my head."

"That made you?"

          "Yes."

                    "Just the moon and the light it made
Under the tree?"

          "Well, your mouth too."

                              "Yes. My mouth?"

"And the quiet there that sang like the drum in the booth.
You shouldn't have danced like that."

                              "Like what?"

                                        "So close,
With your head turned up, and the flower in your hair, a rose
That smelt all warm."

                    "I loved you. I thought you knew
I wouldn't have danced like that with any but you."

"I didn't know. I thought you knew it was fun."

"I thought it was love you meant."

                    "Well, it's done."

                                        "Yes, it's done.
I've seen boys stone a blackbird, and watched them drown
A kitten . . . it clawed at the reeds, and they pushed it down
Into the pool while it screamed. Is that fun, too?"

"Well, boys are like that . . . Your brothers . . ."

                                        "Yes, I know.
But you, so lovely and strong! Not you! not you!"

"They don't understand it's cruel. It's only a game."

"And are girls fun, too?"

                    "No. Still, in a way it's the same.

It's queer and lovely to have a girl . . ."
                                    "Go on."
"It makes you mad for a bit to feel she's your own,
And you laugh and kiss her, and maybe you give her a ring,
But it's only in fun."
                        "But I gave you everything."
"Well, you shouldn't have done it. You know what a fellow thinks
When a girl does that."
                        "Yes, talks of her over his drinks
And calls her a —"
                        "Stop that now, I thought you knew."
"But it wasn't with anyone else. It was only you."
"How did I know? I thought you wanted it too.
I thought you were like the rest — Well, what's to be done?"
"To be done?"
            "Is it all right?"
                            "Yes."
                                    "Sure?"
                                        "Yes, but why?"
"I don't know. I thought you were going to cry.
You said you had something to tell me."
                                    "Yes, I know.
It wasn't anything really. . . . . I think I'll go."
"Yes, it's late. There's thunder about, a drop of rain
Fell on my hand in the dark. I'll see you again
At the dance next week. You're sure that everything's right?"
"Yes."
        "Well, I'll be going."
                        "Kiss me."
                                "Good night."
                                        "Good night."
                                Muriel Stuart (1889–1967)

THE NUN'S LAMENT*
(From the medieval Latin)

A nun is sabbin sairly
She'd deave ye wi her granes
As girnin, greetin rarely
She says ontil her friens:
    "Wae's me!

Nocht could e'er be waur
        Nor sic a life.
I'd raither be a hure
        Or randy wife.

I jow the haly bell,
O psalms I tell my stent.
I'm waukent in my cell
Wi radgie dreams fair spent
        (Wae's me)
To nichtlang vigil keep
        Och sae sweirly,
When wi a man I'd sleep
        Baith late and early."

                                        J. K. Annand (b. 1908)

THE TEMPTATION*

But twa mair steps, and twa alane,
and suddent on the onwytin air
a harem-daunse begins its hetsom tunes
in a siller stramash o wee smaa bells
tinklerin frae queynies' wrists and feet.
And awa ahint them, frae a reithe countrie,
flauntin fiddles pent fey luve's delytes,
and faurder awa, on the rim o kennin,
a mockin flute whilk micht be mou'd by Pan
tuims daurksom lauchin on the seuchin strings.

Attour his heid come braiths o fremit flouers,
pou'd in the gairden whaur the Lilith jaud
thocht oot the weys o hes and shes
and smirked til her lane nainsel;
sic scents o eastlin lemanrie
there's a greinin glent in the prince's ee.

And syne
frae the hert o a dirlin wheesh,
flauntin him, comes the daurk Delilah,
temptation's flame, the sprit o Ashtaroth,
a causey-cantie Aphrodite,
settin afore his een the wiles
o centuries o limmer-lear.

And there he stude,
ay, there he stude, the raucle prince,
in aa the dourness o his weird,
smirkin a wee,
his een fair glinkin at the besom,
bydin her move.

Lang, lang they pree'd ilk ither's een,
hers dark and saft wi devious desires,
his mockin, kennin, blye for aa perchance.
Syne slawlie slawlie she backit awa,
her breists douce jinglin at ilka move,
the while she streikit up her airms
as tho she'd devou the vauntie mune.

Fae ilka clime o cantie limmerheid
she wrings the essence oot in daunse:
for nou she is a yalla birdie
naikit-breistit oot in faur Malay;
and nou she is a skilp fae Zanzibar
leamin black, wi basilisk een;
and nou she is a slee-mou'd French mamselle
wi lear o lewdness gey bezant.
And aa the while throu ilka guiser's pairt,
she's aye mair naikit nir the naikit flesh,
naikit as Eden, wi the kennin forbye.

The prince he stauns like a loon in dwaum,
his een fair thirlit til the shaw,
lauchin laich, a wee areird.

Delilah smirks.
She claps her hauns, and richt awa
her hinnies aa come slitherin oot
wi bottles o wines o aa the airts
o the drucken mappamound,
black anes, reid anes, yalla anes like gowd. . . .
But the prince he grups the usqueba
and tuims a couple o magical mutchkins,
and he and she they clink their glesses
and doun their drams.
And owre his shouther he flings his gless
and breks it til a thoosand diamonts.

Syne owre he lowps and grups Delilah
and birls her aff her naikit feet
(lauchin the while a whinstane lauch),
daunlin her and haunlin her and warsslin tae,
and shawin her the cantrips come his wey
fae bints in black Arabia,
fae bordels in Italian wynds,
fae queynies in the China Seas.
At first she mimped and smirked and seuched;
and syne she gawked and syne she skirled;
and syne she warssled, focht, and scrieched;
and syne she culd but maen. . . .

John Kincaid (1909–1981)

WEARY*

Wearie, wearie nou I dwyne,
I' the westren pend my starne declynes;
Aince enfieft there's nae release
Frae Luve but Strumpet Daith's embrace
  —And sune I maun seek her laillie lair
  Gin my luve winna hae me mair.

I hae seen you Messaline,
—Fata Morgana, to be complimentarie—
Gouned in royal cramasie, wi
Teats o pitch and yalla een
Burnan and burstan, leonine,
Wi a reid wab o veins,
Settan whar the roads cross
Slummoched on her creishie hochs,
A vast Leviathan o Lecherie
Swaulit like a luver's hert
Wi eisenin and an ower-spicie dietarie
               (Hiech-livin and laich-thinkin,
                As sayis the diagnostician)
Aye bydan sans impatience or concern
The current and weirdit aipple o her ee.

  Nane ever flees her, nane
  Escapes, no never ane,
And she can byde, byde three
  Score year and ten,

And mair gif need there be—
I' the end we aa gae doun
   The bricht and fleeran anes,
   The runklit and forworn,
Aa i the end maun gratifie
Her deidlie aye-unstecht desire,
Clipped til her pyson-drappan paps
    O' cauld, cauld alabaister.
—And nou me-ward I see her leer,
      The hure!

Sydney Goodsir Smith (1915–1975)

THE WUMMAN

I'd gie her ma dreams
for a dram o the fouth o her kisses,
but whit daes she offer,
this wurld, this bitch o a wumman?

    Her tongue in its tantrums
    o tepid and tasteless tea temper.

Ma dancin desire
like the banner o gowden hairst growean,
but whit is her blarney,
this wurld, the expedient bitch?

    Here's buits for yer feet,
    noo gang bou yer braid back tae the tatties.

I'd byde in her breists
like the beild o a warm simmer gloamin,
but whaur daes she plant me,
this wurld, this bitch o a wumman?

    Ye'll keep ye mair snod
    gin ye howk yer ain coals, I may tell ye.

I'll get me a lass
that's the lyke o the lilt o the laverock,
whause kisses are gyte
wi the mune and the rants o the randie;

feet licht as the skyre
an the skyte o a widdreme o starnies.

I'll get me a wumman
wha 's hauf o the wurld, or nane o't.

T. S. *Law (b. 1916)*

THE BENEFACTOR

He'd taught her every single thing she knew.
At sixteen plus, he took her maidenhead
Expertly, with the minimum of fuss,
And gave her orgasm on the self-same bed.

Her spirit, like her body, got its due:
Her mind he moulded while her beauty flowered;
Till nothing lacked that he might be so bold
As teach her tolerance, his final dower.

Svengali with Pygmalion might vie,
But Casanova's gift he had to share
With all who offered, novice or adept.

When Galatea, free, gave him the air,
Incredibly, ungratefully, he wept;
Then, as an extra lesson, blacked her eye.

William J. *Tait (b. 1918)*

FADO

Fold those waves away
and take the yellow, yellow bay,
roll it up like Saturday.

No use the sleepy sand,
no use my breasts in his brown hand.
I danced on tables in that land.

Grim is my cold sun.
Through my street the long rains run.
Thousands I see, thinking of one.

Edwin Morgan (b. 1920)

SMOKE

I scratch a gap in the curtains:
the darkest morning of the year
goes grey slowly, chains of orange street-lights
lose out east in Glasgow's haze. The smell
of cigarette smoke fills the bedroom. I drown
in it, I gulp you through my lungs again
and hardly find what can be breathed.
Are you destroying me? Or is it a comedy?
To get together naked in bed, was that all?
To say you had done it? And that we did nothing
was what you had done. Iago and Cassio
had a better night. It must be a laugh
to see us both washed out with lying there.
It doesn't feel like laughing, though,
it feels like gasping, shrieking, tearing, all in silence
as I leave your long curved back
and go through to the kettle and the eggs.

Edwin Morgan (b. 1920)

THE FATHER*

Did she? Did she? I'm really not surprised
I'm really not. Vodka, rum, gin—
some night yon was. Was it me?
Was it my bairn? Christ I don't know,
it might have been, I had her all right—
but there was three of us you know—
at least three—there was big Alec
and the wee French waiter wi the limp
(what d'ye cry him, Louie, wee Louie)—
and we went to this hut down by the loch—
it was a perfect night, perfect night—
mind you, we were all staggering a bit
but she was the worst let me tell you.
Big Alec, he's standing behind her and
kinna nibbling her neck and he leans over
and pulls her breasts out and says What have we here?
and she's giggling with her hair all over the place—
she looked that stupit we were all laughing—
no, I'm telling a lie, we werny all laughing,

I'll aye remember the French kid, Louie,
he wasny laughing, eyes like wee ferrets
as if he'd never seen yon before, and maybe
he hadn't, but he couldny take his eyes off her.
We got in the hut, into the hut
and see her, soon as we were in that door—
out like a light, flat on her back.
Well, I got going, then the other two,
but if you ask me they didny do much,
they'd had a right skinful and they were—
anyhow, I don't remember much after that,
it all goes a bit hazy. But I do remember
coming out the hut it was a lovely night,
it was July and it was a lovely night
with the big trees and the water an all.

Edwin Morgan (b. 1920)

CAMPOBASSO ITALY UNDATED REPORTED MARCH 1971*

Giovanna
handsome, forty,
lazes on the mattress,
her legs are apart, the rumpled sheet
is clutched below her breasts.
With one hand on her swelling child
she is heavy and drowsy as a cat.
Her husband killed himself a year ago.
What will she call this baby then?
She smiles, thinking.

Angelo
her lover, a message-boy of seventeen,
lies sleeping beside her.
His good looks are not quite hidden by the pillow.
He is her son-in-law.
Having made both wife and mother-in-law
pregnant, he sleeps easily.
What insolence you see
in his shrugged strong back!

Antonio
her little grandson
sleeps in his cot at the foot of the bed,

but he will never waken
from the weedkiller his mother has given him.
His arms grip the sides of the cot,
his belly is bent up like a hoop.

Salbina
her daughter, aged fourteen,
seduced by Angelo the year before
while her mother watched and encouraged their play,
can be seen
through the door that opens to the kitchen
swaying from the rafters in a white nightdress
like a dead sea-bird.
With her last convulsion
she has kicked over a table and a smashed wine-bottle
spreads below her like blood.

Gennarino
her nine-year-old son
crouches like a dog in a corner of the farmhouse
unwashed, wide-eyed, afraid to whimper.
No one cares for him but he is the witness
and will sit high in the cold black court.

Edwin Morgan (b. 1920)

MARILYN MONROE STILL 1968*

The substance grins from a skull, the shadow smiles,
The flesh that has long wept from the bones
Glows on the page with a paradise glory,
Immortally golden,
Her sensuous sainthood haloed
By shining sex
That makes her yet the all too mortal world's
Miraculous maiden.

Her beauty's flame
Was fed by the forced draught
That howled from despair,
The emptiness inmost, gibbering void
Of bastard ancestral voices
Denying identity, sneering at sense of self,

Insisting on naked negation,
The falseness of fortune, that fickleness fame,
The uttermost absence of love
For lust's madonna
Shrined in a hell of proxied passions
Where fornicators spat our fantasies
To foul her image.

Those hatreds hurricaned,
Blew out her blaze
With brutal breath.

Alexander Scott (b. 1920)

BALLADE OF BEAUTIES

Miss Israel Nineteen-Sixty-Eight is new,
A fresh-poured form her swimsuit moulds to sleekness,
Legs long, breasts high, the shoulders firm and true,
The waist a lily-wand without a weakness,
The hair, *en brosse* and black, is shorn to bleakness,
Yet shines as stars can make the midnight do—
But still my mind recalls more maiden meekness,
Miss Warsaw Ghetto Nineteen-Forty-Two.

Her masters filmed her kneeling stripped to sue
The mercy barred as mere unmanning weakness,
Or raking rubbish-dumps for crusts to chew,
Or licking boots to prove her slavish meekness,
Or baring loins to lie beneath the bleakness
Of conquerors' lust (and forced to smile it through),
Her starving flesh a spoil preferred to sleekness,
Miss Warsaw Ghetto Nineteen-Forty-Two.

The prize she won was given not to few
But countless thousands, paid the price of meekness,
And paid in full, with far too high a due,
By sadist dreams transformed to functioned sleekness,
A pervert prophet's weakling hate of weakness
Constructing a mad machine that seized and slew,
The grave her last reward, the final bleakness,
Miss Warsaw Ghetto Nineteen-Forty-Two.

Princesses, pale in death or sunned in sleekness,
I dedicate these loving lines to you,
Miss Israel Sixty-Eight and (murdered meekness)
Miss Warsaw Ghetto Nineteen-Forty-Two.

Alexander Scott (b. 1920)

DUO

I

Bathed in her breath I basked beside her, weak
And trembling. She had burst beneath me like
A bomb, her body banging upward, teak-
Hard and beautiful, firm as a spike,
Bold as a bitch . . . and a bitch she was,
Snarling once and tearing more than once;
A beast with blood upon her raking claws.
Below me, slipping from me, not an ounce
Of strength within me, a sudden spasm bent
Her backwards, arching like a bridge. A shudder, a shriek,
Collapse, and for a moment, death. Spent,
My heart insane, without the power to speak,
I could only lie and listen to her breathing:
I could only lie and listen to her breathing.

II

Back to back until the last button tied
Us once again to our anonymity,
Clipped and casual in attempts to hide
The awkwardness of our sterility
In the aftermath's uneasy air, we made
What reparations necessary. Rain
Was pounding on the street outside. My frayed
Hair combed, my collar neat, I tried to train
My tongue to a convincing lie. "I'll come
Again," I said. She didn't show delight
Exactly, but smiled. "Why not! I'm always home
About this time." She knew the signs all right.
We kissed to the sound of my shuffling feet.
Two minutes later, I was on the street.

William Keys (b. 1928)

SONG OF SOLOMON

You
smell nice he said
what is it?
Honey? He nuzzled a soap-trace
in the hollow of her collarbone.
The herbs of her hair?
Salt? He licked
a riverbed between her breasts.

(He'd seemed
not unconvinced by the chemical
attar of roses at her armpit. She tried
to relax have absolute faith in
the expensive secretions of teased civet to
trust the musk at her pulse spots
never think of the whiff of
sourmilk from her navel
the curds of cheese between the toes
the dried blood smell of many small wounds
the stink of fish at her crotch.)

No there he was above her apparently
as happy as a hog rooting for truffles.
She caressed him behind the ear
with the garlic of her cooking-thumb.
She banged shut her eyes
and hoped he would not smell her fear.

Liz Lochhead (b. 1948)

8

Eros Otherwise

THIS HINDIR NYCHT

This hindir nycht in Dumfermeling,
To me was tawld ane windir thing;
That lait ane tod wes with ane lame,
And with hir playit, and maid gud game,
Syne till his breist did hir imbrace,
And wald haif riddin hir lyk ane rame:
And that me thocht ane ferly cace.

He braisit hir bony body sweit,
And halsit hir with fordir feit;
Syne schuk his taill, with quhinge and yelp,
And todlit with hir lyk ane whelp;
Syne lowrit on growfe and askit grace:
And ay the lame cryd, "Lady, help!"
And that me thocht ane ferly cace.

The tod wes nowder lene nor skowry,
He wes ane lusty reid haird lowry,
Ane lang taild beist and grit with all;
The silly lame wes all to small
To sic ane tribbill to hald ane bace:
Scho fled him nocht; fair mot hir fall!
And that me thocht ane ferly cace.

The tod wes reid, the lame wes quhyte,
Scho wes ane morsall of delyte;
He lovit na yowis auld, tuch, and sklender:
Becaus this lame wes yung and tender,
He ran upoun hir with a race,
And scho schup nevir for till defend hir:
And that me thocht ane ferly cace.

He grippit hir abowt the west,
And handlit hir as he had hest;
This innocent, that nevir trespast,
Tuke hert that scho wes handlit fast,
And lute him kis hir lusty face;
His girnand gamis hir nocht agast:
And that me thocht ane ferly cace.

He held hir till him be the hals,
And spak full fair, thocht he wes fals;
Syne said and swoir to hir be God,
That he suld nocht tuich hir prenecod;
The silly thing trowd him, allace!
The lame gaif creddence to the tod:
And that me thocht ane ferly cace.

I will no lesingis put in vers,
Lyk as thir jangleris dois rehers,
Bot be quhat maner thay were mard,
Quhen licht wes owt and durris wes bard;
I wait nocht gif he gaif hir grace,
Bot all the hollis wes stoppit hard:
And that me thocht ane ferly cace.

Quhen men dois fleit in joy maist far,
Sone cumis wo, or thay be war;
Quhen carpand wes thir two most crows,
The wolf he ombesett the hous,
Upoun the tod to mak ane chace;
The lamb than cheipit lyk a mows;
And that me thocht ane ferly cace.

Throw hiddowis yowling of the wowf,
This wylie tod plat doun on growf,
And in the silly lambis skin,
He crap als far as he micht win,
And hid hirn thair ane weill lang space;
The yowis besyd thay maid na din:
And that me thocht ane ferly cace.

Quhen of the tod wes hard no peip,
The wowf went all had bene on sleip;
And, quhill the bell had strikkin ten,
The wowf hes drest him to his den,

Protestand for the secound place:
And this report I with my pen,
How at Dumfermling fell the cace.

William Dunbar (c. 1465–c. 1513)

AN ODE INSCRIBED TO KING WILLIAM*

To hide their pastime from the sun,
   Stretch'd in a gloomy grove,
Alexis lay with Corydon
   Like Ganymede with Jove.

The amorous swain relates with grief
   Love's lamentable story,
And little Alexis gave belief
   To all was told by Cory.

Sighing, said he, "Alone, 'tis you
   Can bless my inclination;"
But what the shepherd meant to do
   Is needless here to mention.

Yet in the sequel, we may find
   The younker was not cruel,
And that a swain so very kind
   Fed not on water-gruel.

Fair Amarylis, passing by,
   A nose had like a terrier;
Soon smelt them out, and saw them lie
   Like Venus with the warrior.

Just as the swain had tun'd his pipe,
   And all his courting ended,
When the love-plot was fully ripe,
   She spoil'd what they intended.

Dire jealousy her rage provok'd
   To most unchristian wishes;
She could have seen Alexis chok'd,
   And Cory torn to pieces!

"Tell me," quoth she, "what do you see
    In him the De'il has sent ye,
But what you know possess'd by me,
    And that in greater plenty.

My buttocks often to your cost,"
    And then she clapt her thigh, Sir,
"And sure your pathick cannot boast
    An arse so fair as I, Sir.

But since 'tis vain for me to rail,
    To make you change your fancy,
I'll in my turn go wag my tail,
    With Chloe's little Nancy.

Think not that we have active maids,
    As you have passive boys, Sir,
To ease us with less dangerous aids,
    And give more lasting joys, Sir."

"Agreed," quoth Cory, "let's embrace;
    Henceforth let nothing vex us,
Go you, take Nancy in my place,
    I'll take in yours Alexis."

Thus parted Corydon with her,
    To whom he once was cully;
And to old Jamie's does prefer
    A mode brought in by Willy.

                        Alexander Robertson (1668–1741)

A BONIE HEN*

'Twas ae night lately, in my fun,
I gaed a rovin wi' the gun,
An' brought a Paitrick to the grun',
        A bonie hen,
And, as the twilight was begun,
            Thought nane wad ken.

The poor, wee thing was little hurt;
I straiket it a wee for sport,
Ne'er thinkan they wad fash me for 't;
   But, Deil-ma-care!
Somebody tells the Poacher-Court
   The hale affair.

Some auld, us'd hands hae taen a note,
That sic a hen had got a shot;
I was suspected for the plot;
   I scorn'd to lie;
So gat the whissle o' my groat,
   An' pay't the fee.

But by my gun, o' guns the wale,
An' by my pouther an' my hail,
An' by my hen, an' by her tail,
   I vow an' swear!
The game shall pay, owre moor an' dail,
   For this, niest year.

As soon 's the clockin-time is by,
An' the wee powts begun to cry,
Lord, I'se hae sportin by an' by,
   For my gowd guinea;
Tho' I should herd the buckskin kye
   For 't, in Virginia!

Trowth, they had muckle for to blame!
'Twas neither broken wing nor limb,
But twa-three draps about the wame
   Scarce thro' the feathers;
An' baith a gowden George to claim,
   An' thole their blethers!

       Robert Burns (1759–1796)

MYTH*

"Men say that the beast delights in the embrace of a virgin, falling asleep in her arms . . . but, awaking, he finds that he is bound." *Natalis Comes*

   A Trochrie wench ca'd Trottie Lee,
   Lang or John Knox was born,

Thocht mebbe her virginity
Wud crib the unicorn.

It was upon a Lammas nicht
She socht him wi' guid-will;
The mune breel'd by, and in its licht
He staig'd attour the hill.

Buff as a mither-naked bairn
She frisk't alang the slack:
The beast cam beckin doun ane's erran'—
But snicherin gaed back.

William Soutar (1898–1943)

WILD OATS

Every day I see from my window
pigeons, up on a roofledge—the males
are wobbling gyroscopes of lust.

Last week a stranger joined them, a snowwhite
pouting fantail,
Mae West in the Women's Guild.
What becks, what croo-croos, what
demented pirouetting, what a lack
of moustaches to stroke.

The females—no need to be one of them
to know
exactly what they were thinking—pretended
she wasn't there
and went dowdily on with whatever
pigeons do when they're knitting.

Norman MacCaig (b. 1910)

TAILPIECE

(In the Rotary Tools trial of 1976, Mrs Grant, according to popular report, was
erroneously referred to through the proceedings as Mrs Grunt.)

O Muse! Some special strength may I be lunt
to sing an *a* that opened up to *u*,

and left a married woman in the stew:
an upright legal tale that should enchunt.
Her cuddly-teddy boss set up the stant.
Nothing was said. Between inviting thighs
tired customers released their free surprise
that tools move readier through accustomed cant.
Corruption's hound was loosed upon the hant:
the victims cringed before its scorching punt.
From careless stroke of pen, what virtue 's bunt?
What credit 's robbed from an industrious frant?
But could the law's impartial truth have munt
to keep poor Anna's grant, forever grunt?

Maurice Lindsay (b. 1918)

ANE O NATURE'S

A real gentleman, he wis.
He gied us fifteen pounds
Jist for feelin us up —
The baith of us;
Twa haunds.

Echty, they said he wis,
But a real gentleman,
Awfy polite.
An undertaker, mebbe —
He hed the haunds for it.

Whan fowk ken ye're sisters —
On the gemme, like —
They affen want a double-act,
An we widna dae that
Noarmally;

But a feel, Jesus!
Naethin wrang wi that, shairly;
Naethin kinky.
An he wis a real gentleman.
No like youz!

William J. Tait (b. 1918)

THE CODPIECE*

I have been in many a tight corner
and kept my head. I cover
a multitude of sins. I have my points.
I am as full of life as an egg is of meat.
I die facing the enemy.
Sometimes I am tricked out with stripes,
fully fashioned, sheeny and gorgeous,
purple and orange, itching to bound in the kermess.
And sometimes the only mound
of the body on the bed.

Edwin Morgan (b. 1920)

CHRISTMAS EVE

Loneliness of city Christmas Eves—
with real stars up there—clear—and stars
on poles and wires across the street, and streaming
cars all dark with parcels, home
to families and the lighted window trees—

I sat down in the bus beside him—white jeans,
black jerkin, slumped with head nodding
in sleep, face hidden by long black hair, hands
tattooed on the four fingers ADEN 1967
and on the right hadn five Christian crosses.
As the bus jerked, his hand fell on my knee,
stayed there, lay heavily and alive
with blue carvings from another world
and seemed to hold me like a claw,
unmoving. It moved. I rubbed my ear
to steal a glance from him, found him
stealing a glance at me. It was not
the jerking of the bus, it was a proposition.
He shook his hair back, and I saw his face
for the first time, unshaven, hardman, a warning
whether in Aden or Glasgow, but our eyes held
while that blue hand burned into my leg.
Half drunk, half sleeping—but half what, half what?
As his hand stirred again, my arm covered it
while the bus jolted round a corner.

''Don't ge' aff tae ah ge' aff.''—But the conductor
was watching, came up and shook him, looked at me.
My ticket was up, I had to leave him sprawled there
with that hand that now seemed so defenceless
lying on the seat I had left. Half down the stair
I looked back. The last thing I saw was Aden
and five blue crosses for five dead friends.

It was only fifteen minutes out of life
but I feel as if I was lifted by a whirlwind
and thrown down on some desert rocks to die
of dangers as always far worse lost than run.

Edwin Morgan (b. 1920)

SAPPHO*

I detest men, their constant spiralling to the centre.
Can they never free their minds of the lust for that vacancy
They seek within us, or see our bodies as other than groupings
Around that negative dull hole? The hoarse pressure
Of their demands is always with them.
Their hands already fumble in my gown, as
They decorously greet me for the first time.

Anguish wrings my heart when I look on her
And I can call to mind no image of comfort
For she is besotted with an alien kind, with man,
Even man, who lays his hand like a benediction
On the world and it burns, it burns through and through:
And where that hand has rested, only ashes remain.

This mind he brings to love twists and turns
His girl in his fancy till she, straight-laced
In the image he has preconceived, itches in every
Pore but still tries to fulfil his bonded longings.

They demand our unrestrained devotion, but their eyes
When they look at us are skinned like a dead cat's.

Is it not enough that they lay their bodies on us
But they must also lay their determined minds
Like a rigid constraining net across the world?

The flawless plastic boys' faces I pass without desire;
Narcissus' flower juts behind the ear of each of them.
Their eyes see only themselves, and themselves in each other.
They turn to us with a sigh and condescension, as necessary
For the purpose but not, oh never, the best. Always
That blurred vision of the self lies in their eyes.
Their taste runs to her who returns the most perfected image.
There is no truth and little passion in them, for they are
Truly blinded, and may not know the world as it is.

The girls like apples falling from the tree
Come to me unbidden, unsought.
I teach the due decorum of a smile,
The mild eloquent pressure of a finger-tip.
At night we comfort one another with equality.
There is no she and he to breach the sweet reciprocal
Circle of our joy.

Robin Hamilton (b. 1945)

9

Eros Explicit

IN SECRET PLACE

In secreit place this hyndir nycht,
I hard ane beyrne say till ane bricht,
"My huny, my hart, my hoip, my heill,
I have bene lang your luifar leill,
And can of yow get confort nane;
How lang will ye with danger deill?
Ye brek my hart, my bony ane!"

His bony beird was kemmit and croppit,
Bot all with cale it was bedroppit,
And he wes townysche, peirt, and gukit;
He clappit fast, he kist, and chukkit,
As with the glaiks he wer ouirgane;
Yit be his feirris he wald have fukkit;
Ye brek my hart, my bony ane!

Quod he, "My hairt, sweit as the hunye,
Sen that I borne wes of my mynnye,
I nevir wowit weycht bot yow;
My wambe is of your lufe sa fow,
That as ane gaist I glour and grane,
I trymble sa, ye will not trow;
Ye brek my hart, my bony ane!"

"Tehe!" quod scho, and gaif ane gawfe,
"Be still my tuchan and my calfe,
My new spanit howffing frae the sowk,
And all the blythness of my bowk;
My sweit swanking, saif yow allane
Na leyd I luiffit all this owk;
Fow leis me that graceles gane."

Quod he, "My claver, and my curldodie,
My huny soppis, my sweit possodie,
Be not oure bosteous to your billie,
Be warme hairtit and not evill willie;
Your heylis, quhyt as the quhalis bane,
Gars ryis on loft my quhillelillie;
Ye brek my hart, my bony ane!"

Quod scho, "My clype, my unspaynit gyane,
With moderis mylk yit in your mychane,
My belly huddrun, my swete hurle bawsy,
My huny gukkis, my slawsy gawsy,
Your musing waild perse ane harte of stane,
Tak gud confort, my grit heidit slawsy,
Fow leis me that graceles gane."

Quod he, "My kyd, my capirculyoun,
My bony baib with the ruch brylyoun,
My tendir girle, my wallie gowdye,
My tyrlie myrlie, my crowdie mowdie;
Quhone that oure mouthis dois meit at ane,
My stang dois storkyn with your towdie;
Ye brek my hairt, my bony ane!"

Quod scho, "Now tak me be the hand,
Welcum! my golk of Marie land,
My chirrie and my maikles munyoun,
My sowklar sweit as ony unyoun,
My strumill stirk, yit new to spane,
I am applyit to your opunyoun;
I luif richt weill your graceles gane."

He gaiff to hir ane apill rubye;
Quod scho, "Gramercye! my sweit cowhubye."
And thai twa to ane play began,
Quhilk men dois call the dery dan;
Quhilk that thair myrthis met baythe in ane.
"Wo is me!" quod scho, "quhair will ye, man?
Bot now I luif that graceles gane."

William Dunbar (c. 1465–c. 1513)

THAIS METAMORPHOSE

In Briareus hudge
Thais wish'd shee might change
Her man, and pray's him herefore not to grudge,
Nor fondly think it strange:
For if (said shee) I might the Parts dispose,
I wish you not an hundreth Armes, nor Hands,
But hundreth Things, like those,
With which Priapus in our Garden stands.

William Drummond (1585–1649)

JOHN ANDERSON, MY JO*

John Anderson, my jo, John,
  I wonder what ye mean,
To lie sae lang i' the mornin',
  And sit sae late at e'en?
Ye'll bleer a' your een, John,
  And why do ye so?
Come sooner to your bed at een,
  John Anderson, my jo.

John Anderson, my jo, John,
  When first that ye began,
Ye had as good a tail-tree,
  As ony ither man;
But now it's waxen wan, John,
  And wrinkles to and fro;
I've twa gae-ups for ae gae-down,
  John Anderson, my jo.

I'm backit like a salmon,
  I'm breastit like a swan;
My wame it is a down-cod,
  My middle ye may span:
Frae my tap-knot to my tae, John,
  I'm like the new-fa'n snow;
And it's a' for your convenience,
  John Anderson, my jo.

O it is a fine thing
  To keep out o'er the dyke;
But it's a meikle finer thing,
  To see your hurdies fyke;
To see your hurdies fyke, John,
  And hit the rising blow;
It's then I like your chanter-pipe,
  John Anderson, my jo.

When ye come on before, John,
  See that ye do your best;
When ye begin to haud me,
  See that ye grip me fast;
See that ye grip me fast, John,
  Until that I cry, "Oh!"
Your back shall crack or I do that,
  John Anderson, my jo.

John Anderson, my jo, John,
  Ye're welcome when ye please;
It's either in the warm bed
  Or else aboon the claes:
Or ye shall hae the horns, John,
  Upon your head to grow;
An' that's the cuckold's malison,
  John Anderson, my jo.

Anonymous (18th century)

O GIN I HAD HER*

O gin I had her,
Ay gin I had her,
O gin I had her,
  Black altho' she be.
I wad lay her bale,
I'd gar her spew her kail;
She ne'er should keep a mail
  Till she dandl'd it on her knee.

Anonymous (18th century)

I'LL HA'E A FIDDLER*

I'll ha'e a fiddler to my goodman
I'll ha'e a fiddler to my goodman
If I dinnae get meat eneugh I'll get play,
And I'll get skeeg about a' the lang day.

Anonymous (18th century)

THE LINKIN' LADDIE*

"Wae's me that e'er I made your bed!
    Wae's me that e'er I saw ye!
For now I've lost my maidenhead,
    An' I ken na how they ca' ye."

"My name's weel kend in my ain countrie,
    They ca' me the linkin' laddie;
An' ye had na been as willing as I,
    Shame fa' them wad e'er hae bade ye."

Anonymous (18th century)

SUPPER IS NA READY*

Roseberry to his lady says,
    "My hinnie and my succour,
O shall we do the thing you ken,
    Or shall we take our supper?"

Wi' modest face, sae fu' o' grace,
    Replied the bonny lady;
"My noble lord do as you please,
    But supper is na ready."

Anonymous (18th century)

HAD I THE WYTE*

Had I the wyte, had I the wyte,
    Had I the wyte she bad me;
For she was steward in the house,
    And I was fit-man laddie;

And when I wadna do't again,
  A silly cow she ca'd me;
She straik't my head, and clapt my cheeks,
  And lous'd my breeks and bad me.

Could I for shame, could I for shame,
  Could I for shame deny her;
Or in the bed was I to blame,
  She bad me lye beside her:
I pat six inches in her wame,
  A quarter wadna fly'd her;
For ay the mair I ca'd it hame,
  Her ports they grew the wider.

My tartan plaid, when it was dark,
  Could I refuse to share it;
She lifted up her holland sark
  And bad me fin' the gair o't:
Or how could I amang the garse,
  But gie her hilt and hair o't;
She clasped her houghs about my arse,
  And ay she glowr'd for mair o't.

Anonymous (18th century)

DUNCAN GRAY*

Can ye play me Duncan Gray,
  Ha, ha, the girdin' o't;
O'er the hills an' far awa,
  Ha, ha, the girdin' o't,
Duncan came our Meg to woo,
Meg was nice an' wadna do,
But like an ither puff'd and blew
  At offer o' the girdin' o't.

Duncan, he cam here again,
  Ha, ha, the girdin' o't,
A' was out, an' Meg her lane,
  Ha, ha, the girdin' o't;
He kiss'd her butt, he kiss'd her ben,
He bang'd a thing against her wame;
But, troth, I now forget its name,
  But, I trow, she gat the girdin' o't.

She took him to the cellar then,
   Ha, ha, the girdin' o't,
To see gif he could do't again,
   Ha, ha, the girdin' o't;
He kiss'd her aince, he kiss'd her twice,
An' by the bye he kiss'd her thrice
Till deil a mair the thing wad rise
   To gie her the long girdin' o't.

But Duncan took her to his wife,
   Ha, ha, the girdin' o't,
To be the comfort o' his life,
   Ha, ha, the girdin' o't;
An' now she scauls baith night an' day,
Except when Duncan's at the play;
And that's as seldom as he may,
   He's weary o' the girdin' o't.

                                Anonymous (18th century)

WAD YE DO THAT?*

"Gudewife, when your gudeman's frae hame,
   Might I but be sae bauld,
As come to your bed-chamber,
   When winter nights are cauld;
As come to your bed-chamber,
   When nights are cauld and wat,
And lie in your gudeman's stead,
   Wad ye do that?"

"Young man, an ye should be so kind,
   When our gudeman's frae hame,
As come to my bed-chamber,
   Where I am laid my lane;
And lie in our gudeman's stead,
   I will tell you what,
He fucks me five times ilka night,
   Wad ye do that?"

                                Anonymous (18th century)

GOWF MY LOGIE*

Of modest maids in simple weeds,
    I've nothing for to say man,
But 'gainst the game of hawking wench,
    I'll tell you and you'll stay man.
            Chorus
And ye busk sae bra lassie,
    And ye busk sae bra,
The lads will crack your maidenhead,
    And that's against the law.

I view them aft come to the church,
    With meal upon their hair man;
Whom I have seen in former times,
    With back and buttocks bare man;
O do not look so high lassie,
    O do not look so high,
You'll mind your mither was but poor,
    Though now ye drink your tea.

Those dirty maids come to the church,
    Holding their mouths as mim man,
Like riddle-rims their tails go round,
    Fine coats stript in the loom man;
O vow but ye be vogie lassie,
    O vow but ye be vogie,
You're proud to wear that whorelike coat,
    It's name is gowf my logie.

                              Anonymous (18th century)

GREEN GROW THE RASHES O*

Green grow the rashes O,
Green grow the rashes O,
The lasses they hae wimble bores,
The widows they hae gashes O.

In sober hours I am a priest;
    A hero when I'm tipsey, O;
But I'm a king and ev'ry thing,
    When wi' a wanton gipsey O.
        Green grow etc.

'Twas late yestreen I met wi' ane,
　　An' wow, but she was gentle, O!
Ae han' she pat roun' my cravat,
　　The tither to my pintle O.
　　　　Green grow etc.

I dought na speak—yet was na fley'd—
　　My heart play'd duntie, duntie, O;
An' ceremony laid aside,
　　I fairly fun' her cuntie O.
　　　　Green grow etc.

Robert Burns (1759–1796)

COME REDE ME, DAME

"Come rede me, dame, come tell me, dame,
　　"My dame come tell me truly,
"What length o' graith, when weel ca'd hame,
　　"Will sair a woman duly?"
The carlin clew her wanton tail,
　　Her wanton tail sae ready—
I learn'd a sang in Annandale,
　　Nine inch will please a lady.—

But for a koontrie cunt like mine,
　　In sooth, we're nae sae gentle;
We'll tak tway thumb-bread to the nine,
　　And that's a sonsy pintle:
O leeze me on my Charlie lad,
　　I'll ne'er forget my Charlie!
Tway roarin handfu's and a daud,
　　He nidge't it in fu' rarely.—

But weary fa' the laithron doup,
　　And may it ne'er be thrivin!
It's no the length that makes me loup,
　　But it's the double drivin.—
Come nidge me, Tam, come nudge me, Tam,
　　Come nidge me o'er the nyvel!
Come lowse and lug your battering ram,
　　And thrash him at my gyvel!

Robert Burns (1759–1796)

THE TAYLOR FELL THRO' THE BED

The taylor fell thro' the bed, thimble an' a',
The taylor fell thro' the bed thimble an' a';
The blankets were thin and the sheets they were sma',
The taylor fell thro' the bed, thimble an' a'.

The sleepy bit lassie she dreaded nae ill,
The sleepy bit lassie she dreaded nae ill;
The weather was cauld and the lassie lay still,
She thought that a taylor could do her nae ill.

Gie me the groat again, cany young man,
Gie me the groat again, cany young man;
The day it is short and the night it is lang,
The dearest siller that ever I wan.

There's somebody weary wi' lying her lane,
There's somebody weary wi' lying her lane,
There's some that are dowie, I trow wad be fain
To see the bit taylor come skipping again.

Robert Burns (1759–1796)

WHA IS THAT AT MY BOWER-DOOR?

Wha is that at my bower-door?
    O wha is it but Findlay;
Then gae your gate, ye'se nae be here!
    Indeed maun I, quo' Findlay.—

What mak ye, sae like a thief?
    O come and see, quo' Findlay;
Before the morn ye'll work mischief;
    Indeed will I, quo' Findlay.—

Gif I rise and let you in,
    Let me in, quo' Findlay;
Ye'll keep me waukin wi' your din;
    Indeed will I, quo' Findlay.—

In my bower if ye should stay,
    Let me stay, quo' Findlay;

I fear ye'll bide till break o' Day;
  Indeed will I, quo' Findlay.—

Here this night if ye remain,
  I'll remain, quo' Findlay;
I dread ye'll learn the gate again;
  Indeed will I, quo' Findlay.—

What may pass within this bower,
  Let it pass, quo' Findlay;
Ye maun conceal till your last hour;
  Indeed will I, quo' Findlay.—

Robert Burns (1759–1796)

BONIE MARY

Chorus

Come cowe me, minnie, come cowe me;
Come cowe me, minnie, come cowe me;
The hair o' my arse is grown into my cunt,
And they canna win to, to mowe me.

When Mary cam over the Border,
When Mary cam over the Border;
As eith 'twas approachin the cunt of a hurchin,
Her arse was in sic a disorder.—

But wanton Willie cam west on't,
But wanton Willie cam west on't,
He did it sae tickle, he left nae as meikle
'S a spider wad bigget a nest on't.—

And was nae Wattie a clinker,
He mow'd frae the Queen to the tinkler,
Then sat down, in grief, like the Macedon chief,
For want o' mae warlds to conquer.—

And O, what a jewel was Mary!
And O, what a jewel was Mary!
Her face it was fine, and her bosom divine,
And her cunt it was theekit wi glory.—

Robert Burns (1759–1796)

ACT SEDERUNT OF THE SESSION

In Edinburgh town they've made a law,
   In Edinburgh at the Court o' Session,
That standing pricks are fauteors a',
   And guilty of a high transgression.—
            Chorus
      Act Sederunt o' the Session,
      Decreet o' the Court o' Session,
      That standing pricks are fauteors a',
      And guilty of a high transgression.

And they've provided dungeons deep,
   Ilk lass has ane in her possession;
Until the wretches wail and weep,
   They there shall lie for their transgression.—

            Chorus
      Act Sederunt o' the Session,
      Decreet o' the Court o' Session,
      The rogues in pouring tears shall weep,
      By act Sederunt o' the Session.

Robert Burns (1759–1796)

ODE TO SPRING

When maukin bucks, at early fucks,
   In dewy glens are seen, sir;
And birds, on boughs, take off their mows,
   Amang the leaves sae green, sir;
Latona's sun looks liquorish on
   Dame Nature's grand impetus,
Till his pengo rise, then westward flies
   To roger Madame Thetis.

Yon wandering rill that marks the hill,
   And glances o'er the brae, sir,
Slides by a bower where many a flower
   Sheds fragrance on the day, sir;
There Damon lay, with Sylvia gay,
   To love they thought no crime, sir;
The wild-birds sang, the echoes rang,
   While Damon's arse beat time, sir.

First, wi' the thrush, his thrust and push
   Had compass large and long, sir;
The blackbird next, his tuneful text,
   Was bolder, clear and strong, sir:
The linnet's lay came then in play,
   And the lark that soar'd aboon, sir;
Till Damon, fierce, mistim'd his arse,
   And fuck'd quite out o' tune, sir.

Robert Burns (1759–1796)

THE BONIE LASS MADE THE BED TO ME

When Januar wind was blawing cauld
   As to the north I took my way,
The mirksome night did me enfauld,
   I knew na whare to lodge till day.—

By my gude luck a maid I met,
   Just in the middle o' my care;
And kindly she did me invite
   To walk into a chamber fair.—

I bow'd fu' low unto this maid,
   And thank'd her for her courtesie;
I bow'd fou' low unto this maid,
   And bade her mak a bed for me.—

She made the bed baith large and wide,
   Wi' twa white hands she spread it down;
She put the cup to her rosy lips
   And drank, "Young man now sleep ye sound."—

She snatch'd the candle in her hand,
   And frae my chamber went wi' speed;
But I call'd her quickly back again
   To lay some mair below my head.—

A cod she laid below my head,
   And served me wi' due respect;
And to salute her wi' a kiss,
   I put my arms about her neck.—

Haud aff your hands young man, she says,
    And dinna sae uncivil be:
Gif ye hae ony luve for me,
    O wrang na my virginitie!—

Her hair was like the links o' gowd,
    Her teeth were like the ivorie,
Her cheeks like lillies dipt in wine,
    The lass that made the bed to me.—

Her bosom was the driven snaw,
    Twa drifted heaps sae fair to see;
Her limbs the polish'd marble stane,
    The lass that made the bed to me.—

I kiss'd her o'er and o'er again,
    And ay she wist na what to say;
I laid her between me and the wa',
    The lassie thought na lang till day.—

Upon the morrow when we rase,
    I thank'd her for her courtesie:
But ay she blush'd, and ay she sigh'd,
    And said, Alas, ye've ruin'd me.—

I clasp'd her waist, and kiss'd her syne,
    While the tear stood twinklin in her e'e;
I said, My lassie, dinna cry,
    For ye ay shall mak the bed to me.—

She took her mither's holland sheets
    And made them a' in sarks to me:
Blythe and merry may she be,
    The lass that made the bed to me.—

The bonie lass made the bed to me.
    The braw lass made the bed to me;
I'll ne'er forget till the day that I die
    The lass that made the bed to me.—

                                    Robert Burns (1759–1796)

THE REEL O' STUMPIE

Wap and rowe, wap and row,
  Wap and row the feetie o't,
I thought I was a maiden fair,
  Till I heard the greetie o't.

My daddie was a fiddler fine,
  My minnie she made mantie O;
And I mysel a thumpin quine,
  And danc'd the reel o' Stumpie O.

Robert Burns (1759–1796)

THE PATRIARCH

As honest Jacob on a night,
  Wi' his beloved beauty,
Was duly laid on wedlock's bed,
  And noddin' at his duty:
      Tal de lal, &c.

"How lang, she says, ye fumblin' wretch,
  "Will ye be fucking at it?
"My eldest wean might die of age,
  "Before that ye could get it.

"Ye pegh, and grane, and groazle there,
  "And mak an unco splutter,
"And I maun ly and thole you here,
  "And fient a hair the better."

Then he, in wrath, put up his graith,
  "The deevil 's in the hizzie!
"I mow you as I mow the lave,
  "And night and day I'm bisy.

"I've bairn'd the servant gypsies baith,
  "Forby tour titty Leah;
"Ye barren jad, ye put me mad,
  "What mair can I do wi' you.

"There's ne'er a mow I've gi'en the lave,
    "But ye ha'e got a dizzen;
"And damn'd a ane ye'se get again,
    "Altho' your cunt should gizzen."

Then Rachel calm, as ony lamb,
    She claps him on the waulies,
Quo' she, "ne'er fash a woman's clash,
    "In trowth, ye mow me braulies.

"My dear 'tis true, for mony a mow,
    "I'm your ungratefu' debtor;
"But ance again, I dinna ken,
    "We'll aiblens happen better."

Then honest man! wi' little wark,
    He soon forgat his ire;
The patriarch, he coost his sark,
    And up and till 't like fire!!!

                                Robert Burns (1759–1796)

THE TROGGER

As I cam down by Annan side,
    Intending for the border,
Amang the Scroggie banks and braes
    Wha met I but a trogger.
He laid me down upon my back.
    I thought he was but jokin,
Till he was in me to the hilts,
    O the deevil tak sic troggin!

What could I say, what could I do,
    I bann'd and sair misca'd him,
But whiltie-whaltie gae'd his arse
    The mair that I forbade him:
He stell'd his foot against a stane,
    And doubl'd ilka stroke in,
Till I gaed daft amang his hands,
    O the deevil tak sic troggin!

Then up we raise, and took the road,
   And in by Ecclefechan,
Where the brandy-stoup we gart it clink,
   And the strang beer ream the quech in.
Bedown the bents o' Bonshaw braes,
   We took the partin' yokin';
But I've claw'd a sairy cunt synsine,
   O the deevil tak sic troggin!

Robert Burns (1759–1796)

WHY SHOULD NA POOR FOLK MOWE

When princes and prelates and het-headed zealots
   All Europe hae set in a lowe,
The poor man lies down, nor envies a crown,
   And comforts himsel with a mowe.—

Chorus
And why shouldna poor folk mowe, mowe, mowe,
   And why shouldna poor folk mowe:
The great folk hae siller, and houses and lands,
   Poor bodies hae naething but mowe.—

When Brunswick's great Prince cam a cruising to France
   Republican billies to cowe,
Bauld Brunswick's great Prince wad hae shown better sense,
   At hame with his Princess to mowe.—

Out over the Rhine proud Prussia wad shine,
   To spend his best blood he did vow;
But Frederic had better ne'er forded the water,
   But *spent* as he docht in a mowe.—

By sea and by shore! the Emperor swore,
   In Paris he'd kick up a row;
But Paris sae ready just leugh at the laddie
   And bade him gae tak him a mowe.—

Auld Kate laid her claws on poor Stanislaus,
   And Poland has bent like a bow:
May the deil in her arse ram a huge prick o' brass!
   And damn her in hell with a mowe!

But truce with commotions and new-fangled notions,
    A bumper I trust you'll allow:
Here's George our gude king and Charlotte his queen,
    And lang may they tak a gude mowe!

Robert Burns (1759–1796)

WHA'LL MOW ME NOW

O wha'll mow me now, my jo,
    And wha'll mow me now:
A sodger wi' his bandileers
    Has bang'd my belly fu'.

O, I hae tint my rosy cheeks,
    Likewise my waste sae sma';
O wae gae by the sodger lown,
    The sodger did it a'.

Now I maun thole the scornfu' sneer
    O' mony a saucy quine;
When, curse upon her godly face,
    Her cunt's as merry 's mine.

Our dame hauds up her wanton tail,
    As due as she gaes lie;
An' yet misca's a young thing
    The trade if she but try.

Our dame can lae her ain gudeman,
    And mow for glutton greed;
An' yet misca's a young thing
    That 's mowin' for its bread.

Alake! sae sweet a tree as love,
    Sic bitter fruit should bear!
Alake, that e'er a merry arse,
    Should draw a sa'tty tear.

But deevil damn the lousy loun,
    Denies the bairn he got!
Or lea's the merry arse he lo'ed
    To wear a ragged coat!

Robert Burns (1759–1796)

GIE THE LASS HER FAIRIN'

O gie the lass her fairin', lad,
  O gie the lass her fairin',
An' something else she'll gie to you,
  That 's waly worth the wearin';
Syne coup her o'er amang the creels,
  When ye hae taen your brandy,
The mair she bangs the less she squeels,
  An' hey for houghmagandie.

Then gie the lass her fairin', lad,
  O gie the lass her fairin',
An' she'll gie you a hairy thing,
  An' of it be na sparin';
But coup her o'er amang the creels,
  An' bar the door wi' baith your heels,
The mair she gets the less she squeels;
  An' hey for houghmagandie.

Robert Burns (1759–1796)

LOVE À LA MODE*

See how the poet, fired with love divine,
swives in the barley, full of barley wine,
whilst in the lane, impassioned by Five Star,
some lawyer's at it in his Jaguar.

Robert Garioch (1909–1981)

Notes

Page 25. 'Sensuality.' A speech from Lyndsay's morality play, *The Three Estates*, in which Sensualitie—a personification of illicit sex—seduces the hero from the paths of rectitude until he is redirected there by the spirit of religious reformation. The text, first published in 1602, is of the Edinburgh production of 1554, when the play was performed in the open air to an audience which included the Queen Regent, her courtiers, and "an exceeding great number of people".

Page 26. 'Cupid and Venus'. Boyd was an outstanding poet in Latin. His only extant poem in Scots is this, the greatest of Renaissance sonnets from Scotland.

Page 26. 'Girl Goddess'. The most accomplished of Scotland's seventeenth-century aristocratic poets, Drummond included this madrigal (untitled) in his sequence of love poems published in 1614/15. "The Idalian Queen" is Venus, so-called from the town of Idalium in Cyprus, which was sacred to her. According to legend, the rose sprang from the blood of Venus. The conceit in the concluding lines derives from a sonnet by the Italian poet, Marino.

Page 26. 'Leg-Man'. From 'The Vision', ll. 37–66, written while Burns was still farming in Ayrshire and courting Jean Armour.

Page 27. 'The Advent of Aphrodite'. From 'A Ballad in Blank Verse of the Making of a Poet', ll. 103–26, ll. 143–7, and ll. 194–6. First published in *Ballads and Songs* (1894). "Cyprian" refers to Aphrodite's birth from the sea off the coast of Cyprus, and her "zone" is the girdle which has the power of making everyone fall in love with its wearer. Legend has it that after the death of her lover, Adonis, Aphrodite reclaimed him from the underworld during the summer months. The "noisome port" is Greenock, where Davidson spent his adolescence. The poet's glorification of Greek myth is counterpointed, in the complete poem, against his repudiation of Scottish Calvinism.

Page 29. 'Harry Semen'. MacDiarmid intended this poem for his collection *Stony Limits* (Gollancz, London, 1934), but it was banned by the publisher.

Page 31. 'The Young Audh'. From MacDiarmid's autobiography, *Lucky Poet* (Methuen, 1943). In making this version of Rilke's poem on the birth of Venus, MacDiarmid glorifies one of the heroines of his own personal mythology, Audh the Deep-Minded, a figure of the Viking heroic age who was successively queen in Dublin, landowner in the Scottish Highlands, and settler in Iceland.

Page 34. 'Mars and Venus at Hogmanay'. Part VI of the seven-part sequence 'Armageddon in Albyn' in *The Deevil's Waltz* (Glasgow, 1946). 'The Ball o Kirriemuir' is the most famous, and not the least filthy, of pornographic Scottish folksongs.

II: *Eros Calvinized*

Page 37. 'The Marrow Ballad'. Composed in 1738, when Ramsay's hostility towards Presbyterian extremism had been exacerbated by the attempts of the Edinburgh Presbytery to use the Licensing Act of 1737 in order to force the closure of the theatre which he had opened in the city in 1736. The extremist sect to which the poem refers derived its name from a seventeenth-century work of Calvinist theology, *The Marrow of Modern Divinity*, which was reissued in Scotland in 1718. Erskine and Mair were ministers of the sect. Ramsay's verse, and his correspondence, during the legal process concerning his theatre, when he suffered financial loss, express his rage and contempt for the hypocrisy of Calvinist puritanism.

Page 38. 'Godly Girzy'. One of Burns's contributions to the bawdy collection *The Merry Muses of Caledonia*, first published anonymously *c*. 1800.

Page 38. 'A Tale of a Wife'. Also contributed to *The Merry Muses of Caledonia*. The theological view that it was impossible for one of the "saved" ever again to be guilty of sin is similar to that expressed in James Hogg's superb novel on Calvinist fanaticism, *The Private Memoirs and Confessions of a Justified Sinner* (1824).

Page 40. 'Holy Willie'. From 'Holy Willie's Prayer', ll. 37–60. Burns tells us that "Holy Willie was a rather oldish bachelor elder in the parish of Mauchline, and much and justly famed for that polemical chattering which ends in tippling orthodoxy, and for that spiritualized bawdry which refines to liquorish devotion." First printed anonymously in 1789.

Page 40. 'The Annunciation'. 'The Thistle in the Wind', 'I Wish I Kent'.

Extracted from MacDiarmid's extended masterpiece *A Drunk Man Looks at the Thistle* (Edinburgh, 1926).

Page 46. 'Pffff'. Mr Leonard aims at a phonetic rendering of Glasgow proletarian speech.

III: Eros Bewitching

Page 49. 'Tam Lin'. This version of one of the greatest Scottish supernatural ballads was contributed by Burns to the influential song collection *The Scots Musical Museum*, edited by the Edinburgh engraver James Johnson (*c.* 1750–1811).

Page 54. 'Cutty Sark'. From 'Tam o' Shanter', ll. 163–190.

Page 55. 'May of the Moril Glen'. First published in *Blackwood's Magazine* (1827) as 'The Perils of Wemyng' (Women), an ambiguous title which may be interpreted as meaning either the dangers suffered, or those inflicted, by the female sex. Published under the present title in *A Queer Book* (1832). The last twelve stanzas have been omitted here.

Page 65. 'The Witch's Ballad'. Like his friend Dante Gabriel Rossetti, Scott was both painter and poet. His affinities with Pre-Raphaelitism are evident.

Page 68. 'Bride'. From *A Drunk Man Looks at the Thistle* (1926).

Page 69. 'The Tryst'. A personal expression of motifs from traditional ballads of the supernatural, particularly 'The Wife of Usher's Well'.

Page 70. 'Love is a Garth'. A song, with music by Cedric Thorpe Davie, from the radio verse-play *The Jerusalem Farers* (1950).

IV: Eros Exultant

Page 75. 'The Squire and The Lady'. From the biographical romance *The Historie of Squyer William Meldrum*, ll. 895–1,026.

Page 78. 'My Hairt is Heich'. From the Bannatyne Manuscript, 1568, compiled by George Bannatyne (1546–*c.* 1608).

Page 79. 'Up, Helsum Hairt'. The first Alexander Scott was a professional musician as well as a poet, and may have composed the music for some of his songs.

Page 80. 'Blest'. Dr M. M. Gray, in her *Scottish Poetry from Barbour to James VI* (1935), suggests the possibility that this poem is the work of Drummond of Hawthorden's maternal uncle, William Fowler (1560-1612).

Page 80. Semple was the son of Robert Semple (*c.* 1590–*c.* 1660), whose poem 'The Life and Death of Habbie Simson, the Piper of Kilbarchan' provided a model, and a stanza form—"standard Habbie", later known as "the Burns stanza"—for eighteenth-century humorous elegies in Scots, most notably those of Ramsay, Robert Fergusson and Burns.

Page 82. 'The Fornicator' and 'The Rantin Dog' were written when Burns had become a father for the first time, without benefit of clergy. "Betsy" was Elizabeth Paton, the Burns family's servant-girl.

Page 84. 'Libel Summons' was written for 'The Court of Equity', a secret bachelors' association whose members met sporadically at the Whitefoord Arms Inn, Mauchline, "to search out, report and discuss the merits and demerits of the many scandals that crop up from time to time in the village." The self-appointed 'officers' of the court were all wild young men at the time.

Page 89. 'The Fine Fechtin Moose'. Translated from a Dutch folksong, and first collected in Gray's *Sir Halewyn* (Edinburgh, 1949).

Page 90. 'Solipsist'. This omits the first fifteen lines of the ninth poem of Goodsir Smith's major sequence, *Under the Eildon Tree: a Poem in XXIV Elegies* (Edinburgh, 1948; revised edition, 1954), the most remarkable extended love poem in Scots.

Page 91. Mr Tait is the most notable contemporary poet writing, as here, in the Shetland dialect of Scots.

V: Eros Enraptured

Page 101. 'Love at First Sight'. From *The Kingis Quair*, ll. 267-287 and ll. 302–348. The poem is considered to reflect the experience of King James I of Scotland, who was captured and imprisoned by the English as a youth and later returned to his native country with an English bride. Here the hero, in prison, has his first view of the heroine.

Page 104. 'My Weird is Comforted'. From *Songs from Carmina Burana* (Loanhead, Midlothian, 1978).

VI: Eros Exploited

Page 123. 'Lucky Spence's Last Advice'. Ramsay describes his protagonist as "a famous bawd who flourished for several years about the beginning of the eighteenth century; she had her lodgings near Holyroodhouse. She made a benefit night to herself by putting a trade in the hands of young lasses that had a little pertness, strong passions, abundance of laziness, and no forethought." He glosses l. 41, "Delate them to the Kirk-Trasurer [official responsible for disciplining whores and their customers]. *Hale the dools* is a phrase used at football, where the party that gains the goal or dool is said to hail it or win the game, and so draws the stake."

Page 126. Elegy XIII of *Under the Eildon Tree,* omitting ll. 25-95.

Page 129. 'Fat Marget's Ballade'. Written in Shetland dialect.

Page 130. 'Soho'. From the sequence 'London' in *From Glasgow to Saturn* (Cheadle, Cheshire, 1973).

Page 132. 'The Fan'. From the sequence 'Ten Theatre Poems' in *The New Divan* (Manchester, 1977).

VII: Eros Decried/Denied

Page 137. 'Robene and Makyne'. A satirical contrast between the conventions of the medieval courtly code of love and actuality.

Page 140. 'Repudiation'. From *The Testament of Cresseid,* ll. 71-84 and ll. 113–140. This poem is Henryson's sequel to Chaucer's *Troylus and Cresseid.*

Page 146. 'Blinded Lovers'. The last nine stanzas have been omitted.

Page 148. 'Whoredom'. From 'Auld Reekie', ll. 87–97.

Page 151. 'The Nun's Lament'. From *Songs from Carmina Burana.*

Page 152. 'The Temptation'. From the extended poem *The Prince* (Glasgow, 1952), omitting the last eighteen lines of this section.

Page 154. 'Weary'. Elegy XVIII of *Under the Eildon Tree.*

Page 157. 'The Father'. From the sequence 'Stobhill' in *From Glasgow to Saturn.*

Page 158. 'Campobasso Italy Undated Reported March 1971'. From *Instamatic Poems* (London, 1972). The poems in this collection are presented as the verbal equivalents of the photographs which might have accompanied newspaper reports.

Page 159. 'Marilyn Monroe Still 1968'. Marilyn Monroe died from a drug overdose in 1962.

VIII: Eros Otherwise

Page 167. 'Ode Inscribed to King William'. King William (of Orange) was reputedly homosexual, whereas the father-in-law he supplanted, King James VII and II, was a notorious whoremonger. Alexander Robertson was a political supporter of the latter's cause.

Page 168. 'A Bonie Hen'. From 'Epistle to John Rankine', ll. 37–72. The "hen" was the Burns family's servant-girl, Elizabeth Paton, who bore the poet an illegitimate daughter in 1785.

Page 169. 'Myth'. The unicorn was Soutar's favourite symbol of Scotland, and he regarded with contempt the myth that the legendary beast's potency could be nullified through contact with a female virgin.

Page 172. 'The Codpiece'. From the sequence 'Ten Theatre Poems'.

Page 173. 'Sappho'. First published in *Scottish Poetry 8*, ed. M. Lindsay, A. Scott and R. Watson (Cheadle, Cheshire, 1975). The last three sections of the poem have been omitted.

IX: Eros Explicit

Page 179. 'John Anderson, My Jo'. 'O Gin I Had Her'. From *The Merry Muses of Caledonia*.

Page 181. 'I'll Ha'e a Fiddler'. From the St Clair Manuscript, *c.* 1781/5.

Page 181. 'The Linkin' Laddie'. 'Supper is na Ready', "Had I the Wyte', 'Duncan Gray', 'Wad Ye Do That?' From *The Merry Muses of Caledonia*.

Page 184. 'Gowf My Logie'. From an eighteenth-century chapbook.

Page 184. 'Green Grow the Rashes O' and the other poems by Burns, cf. his letter to Robert Cleghorn, 25th October 1793: "There is, there must be, some truth in original sin. My violent propensity to Bawdy convinces me of it. Lack a day! if that species of Composition be the Sin against the Holy Ghaist, I am the most offending soul alive."

Page 195. 'Love à la Mode'. Another example of the syndrome described elsewhere by the present editor.

SCOTCH SEX
In atween
Drinks.

"Five-Star" is a superior brand of brandy.

Glossary

a', *aa*, all
aathing, everything
abaisit, abashed
abate, shock
abaw, abash
aben, inside
ablow, below
aboon, *abune*, above
aboucht, bought
ae (bit), one (small)
a forrow, before
agee, awry
aiblins, perhaps
aingins, *ingins*, onions
air, early
airt, direction
aith, oath
aix, axe
all-utterly, entirely
als, also
alyte, a little
ain, own
amaille, enamel
amorettis, love-knots
ane, a, one
ane's errand, exclusive errand
aport, bearing
areird, backward
arg, eager
art, witchcraft
ask, adder
astert, started
attour, out-over
aver, old horse
avoir, cart-horse

awcht, owns
ay(e), yes
aye, always
ayont, beyond

bace, bass
bade, remained
baid, waiting
bair, bore
bairn, *barne*, child
baith, both
balas, rubies
bale, sorrow
ban, curse
band, bond
bang, copulate vigorously
barley-wine, whisky
barrat, harm
bask, unpleasant
bauchles, documents
baudrons, cat
ba(u)ld, bold
bawch, worthless
bawaw, scornful glance
be, about the fact that
beal, fester
beck, do obeisance
bedlar, grave-digger
beild, suppurated
belly huddron, glutton
belyf, *belyve*, at once, soon
ben, through
bent, heath
bernis, men, mankind
besom, loose woman

beswick, cheat
betawcht, give
beuche, bough
bezant, brilliant
bield, shelter
bien, comfortable, cosy
bide, byde, remain
bigg(in), build(ing)
biggonet, linen cap or coif
billie, comrade
birs, hairs
blae, ghastly
blash, spurt
blate, bashful
blee, complexion
bleeze, blaze
blenche ferme, free tenure
blenk, wink
blent, glanced, leered
block, copulate
blooster, storm
blue-boram, pox
blynis, ceases
bo, make a face
boel, settle down
bogill, spectre
boordly, sturdy
boot, comfort
bourd, joke
boure bourding, bedroom jesting
bosteous, violent
bowdyn, swollen
bowk, body
bowster, bolster
brae, hill-slope
braid, broad; hurried
braist, embraced
brand, muscled
brank, swagger
brats, rags, clothing
braulies, finely
braw, fine
bree, brow
breeks, trousers
breel, move rapidly
breid, broad; bread
breif, write
breir, grow, flourish

brod, prod
bruck, broken remnants
brukill, frail
brunt, brynt, burned
bryght, beauty
brym, fierce
budd, bribe
buff, bare
bukky, tongue
bumbart, drone
burach, group, crowd
busk, dress
but, without; outside
bute, help
buthman, stall-keeper
by-job, fornication

ca', call; drive, urge forward
cabeld, haltered
cack, excrete upon
caf, chaff
caird, vagrant
cair weed, mourning clothes
caller, fresh
cant, hypocrisy
cantrip, magical trick
canty, lively, cheerful
capirculyon, capercaillie
cappill, horse
carle, fellow
carlin, old woman, witch
carp, chat
carry, mist
carybald, cannibal
cassin, cast
cauld, cold
causy, street
chaft, cheek
chaip, escape
chalmer, chamber, bedroom
chalmer glew, bedroom fun
chap, knock, thrash, beat
chawcht, catch
cheip, squeak
chevist, deeded
chiel, lad, young fellow, chap
chift, shift, remove
chirm, noise of water rippling

chuckie-stane, pebble
chuf, churl
chymys, mansion
clag, claim
claiss, (bed)clothes
claith, cloth
clart, clort, filth, dirt
clatter upon my creed, repeat the Creed continuously
claver, clover
cleek, link arms in a dance; catch as with a hook
cleir, beautiful, peerless
clishmaclavers, wordy discourse
clockin-time, hatching-time, child-bearing
clour, strike
clud, cloud
clype, big soft fellow
cod, pillow
coft, bought
connach, destroy
coof, fool, clown, lout
coorse, wicked
coost, cast off
corp, body
cossis, interchanges
cotts, skirts, petticoats
cought, could
coup, cowp, upset
cour, cower, fold
cout, colt
cowe, crop, trim (the hair)
cowhuby, booby
cowp, cup
cowth, could
crabit, offended
crack, chat jestingly
cramasie, cramoisie, scarlet cloth
crap, crept
creepie stool, chair of repentance in church
creesh, fat, grease
crouse, merry
crummock, crook
cry, call
crynd, withered, shrunken
cuist, cast
cuit, ankle
cumar, neighbour

cummerans, encumbrance
cunyar, coiner
curch, kerchief
curiouslie, carefully
curldoddie, plant
curyus, cared for
cull, testicle
cunt(ie), pudenda
cuschett, cushat dove
cutty, short.

dad, fall
daff, frolic, flirt
daill, dealings
daine, haughty
dam, piss
dandily, like a spoiled woman
dantonie, subdued
darg, work, toil
dauphin, dolphin
daur, dare
daut, caress tenderly
daw, dawn
deaf-nits, something to be dismissed
degest, properly adjusted
denkest, sauciest
dern(e), secret
dery dan, fornication
dill, relieve
ding, knock
dink, trimly
dirkin, eavesdrop
dirl, throb, pang
div, do
dog-hank, dog-knot (in mating)
dogon, worthless fellow
dollin, delved
dolly, woeful
donkit, moistened
doo, dow, dove
doolie, miserable
dortie, conceited
doup, dowp, backside
dour, unrelenting
dow, be able
dowf, mournful, lacking vivacity
dowy, sad
draunt, drivel

dre(e), injure, suffer
drowrie, token
drucken, drunken
drumlie, dull
dry-bob, coitus interruptus
duddies, clothes, rags, tatters
dulce, sweet
dule, misery
dunt, blow
dwaum, dream
dwyne, shrink
dyvor, bankrupt

ee, eye
een, eyen, eyes
eident, eager
eisenin, lustful
eith, easy
eke, increase; also
eldnyng, jealousy
emrod, emerald
engyne, intelligence, imagination
erd, earth
erne, eagle
espyis, witnesses
excambion, exchange
exeme, examine

facture, shape
faem, foam
fairheid, beauty
fairin, reward, deserts, punishment
fand, found
fang, take, seize
farcy, diseased
fash, bother, trouble
fauteour, wrongdoer
fe, sheep
fecht, fight
fefill, fidget
feid, feud, enmity
feill, many
feir, behaviour
fenyeitlie, pretendedly
ferly, ferliful, wonder(ful)
fessoun, fashion, style
feulis, birds
fidge, shrug, twitch (with excitement)

fient the, the devil a
fike, fyke, be uneasy
file, defile
flannen, flannel
fleeman's-firth, outlaw's sanctuary
fleische, flatter
flewme, phlegm
fl(e)y'd, frightened
flichtmafletherie, frippery, trifles
flouer, flower
flyrit, leered
flytin, scolding
fone, fawn
fordir, fare
forenent, opposite, against
forky fure, man of stamina
forleit, abandon
forsy, strong
fortunait, ordained
foryhet, forget
fou, very, full; drunk
fow leis, very dear is
frane, insist
freke, man
fremd, foreign
fret-wise, for adornment
frig, masturbate
fruster, useless
furght, forth

gae(d), go, went
gair, patch, crease
gam, gum
gamphrell, fool
gane, face, suit
ganest, superior
gang, go
gangrel, wanderer, vagrant
gant, yawn
gar(t), make, made
garf, ? deerhound
garth, garden
gate, way
gaud, goad
gawfe, guffaw
gawn, going
gawsy, gall-bladder
gean, cherry

gear, gier, goods
geg, deception
geit, jest
gent, beautiful
gentrice, ladylike
gestis, tales
gib, tom-cat
gie, give
gied, gave; went
gif, if
gigotlike, wantonly
gillot, man
girdin, striking (euphemism)
gizzen, shrivel through drought
gladernt, encrusted
glaik, fool; optical illusion
glamourie, magic
gla(u)r, mud, filth
gleg, glig, sharp
gleid, gloed, flame
glink, gleam
glit, slime
gloaming, twilight
glow(e)r, stare wide-eyed, scowl
glowffin, glare
golk, gowk, fool
goreis, matter
gowd, gold
gowf my logie, strike my hole
grain, grane, groan
graith, tool
gra(i)thit, attired
greet, weep
greinin, longing
grew, greyhound
groanin maut, ale provided for visitors at a lying-in
groat, threepence Scots
groazle, grunt
gubernator, governor
gucking, trifling, fooling
gudeman, husband
gyane, giant
gymp, jimp, neat, delicately
gyte, mad
gyvel, pudenda

hache, ache

hafflins, in half measure
hail, small shot
haill, whole
hair, grey, hoary
hale the dools, hit the mark
halok, foolish
hals, heyls, throat
halsit, embraced
Hangy, the Devil, the hangman
hanyt, retained
harns, brains
hap, cover
hauflin, adolescent
havers, nonsense
heal, heill, health
hechar, higher
hecht, promise
heddir-cowes, clumps of heather
heich, high
heidsman, executioner
heildit, hidden
heist, hoist
hely, highly
herle, heron
herns an wallawa, violent uproar
hete, fever
heuch, cliff
heuchle-bane, hip-bone
heynd, sheltering: gentle; person
hindir, recent
hinney, honey (sweet)
hint, clasped
hird, protect
hizzie, hussy
hoch, thigh
hogeart, ? twitcher
holyn, holly
holt, thicket
hoo, dogfish
hoorhoose, brothel
Hornie, the Devil
host, cough
hotch, jerk about
hotter, simmer
houghmagandie, fornication
hoven, distended
howffing, clumsy fellow
howk(it), dig, dug

huke, frock
hurdies, buttocks
hurchin, hedgehog
hure, whore
hurle bawsy, big soft turd
hy, haste

ilk, each
ingangs, entrails
ingenerit, engendered
ingle-lowe, firelight
in staige, aloft
intent, thought
inthrang, pressed in

janglour, tell-tale
jink, dodge
jo, sweetheart
jock, private soldier in a Scottish regiment
jonettis, the great St John's wort
josit, enjoyed
jott, strut about
jow, ring (bell)

kail, colewort or cabbage soup
kaim, comb
keep, heed
ken, know
kenrick, kingdom
kerffis, bows
kirk, church
kirsp, light, diaphanous fabric
kist, chest
kittle, tickle
knaip, knave, boy
knap, knee
kytch, upward shove
kythis, reveals
kye, cows
kyvel, thump

laich, low
laillie, loathsome, foul
lair, grave
laith, loath
laithron, lazy, inactive, sluggish
laitis, manners, habits
land, tenement

lane, lone; conceal
lammer, amber
lap, lowp, leap
larbar, impotent lover
lave, remainder
laverock, lark
lay her bale, put down her bundle
le(e), lie
leal, leill, loyal
leir, learn(ing)
leman, lover
lemyng, shining
lesing, falsehood
lesum, lawful
let, hindrance
lettis, pretends
leuch, laughed
leyd, man, lover
lichtly, slight
lift, sky
lig(g), lie
limmer, rascal, jade, mistress, whore
link, trip, skip, twine arms
liver-muggies, fish-livers cooked in the
  swim-bladder
lob, clumsy
loffit, praised
loik, lukewarm
loof, palm of the hand
loon, lowne, boy, villain, fool
loppin, leapt upon
losinger, deceiver
louse, lowse, loose
lout, lowt, stoop
lowe, blaze
lowrit, bowed, bent
lowry, fox
lude, loved
luely, gently
lufer, luifer, lover
lug, ear
lum, chimney
lumbart, Lombard (banker)
lume, tool (penis)
lustless, unhappy
lusum, loveable
lydder, idle
lyre, skin

lyth, listen
lythe, flexible

maculait, stained
maen, *mane*, moan
maik, mate
maikles(s), matchless
mail, fee for fornication
mangit, crazy
mantil, gown
mappamound, world
mard, confounded
Marie land, elfland, fairyland
maugre, uneasiness
maukin, hare
maun, must
mavis, thrush
meikle, *muckle*, much
mell, mingle, mate
mense, discretion
mensk, honour, manhood
mercat, market
merrans, wretchedness
miminy, affectedly modest
minnie, mother
mirk, dark
miscuke, miscook
mixter-maxter, part this, part that
moericks, edible roots
molet, bridle bit
mool in, copulate
mools, earth of the grave
moose, mouse
mow(e), copulate
moy, tame
munyoun, minion
mutchkin, English pint

na, *no*, then
nae, no
nainsel, own self
nam, grab
neiff, fist
neist, next
neuk, corner
nidge, thrust, push
noy, annoyance
nyvel, navel

ocht, *oucht*, anything
ombesett, beset
on far, afar
on growf, downwards, prone
on the gemme, whoring
onwytin, awaiting
or, *ere*, before
orra, rubbishy
oulkis, weeks
our, *ower*, *owre*, over
ourhailit, overcome
outwaill, outcast
owk, week
oxster, armpit

paitrick, partridge
pako, peacock
panton, slipper
papingay, parrot
partye, prize
peerie, little, trifling
pedder, pedlar
pegh, pant
pend, arch
pengo, penis
perfyte, perfect
peronall, young girl
pert, sexually mature, attractive
pertlyar, livelier
phizz, countenance
pintle, penis
plack, penny-piece
plag, garment
plane, *plene*, complain
plenished, furnished
ploy, game
poosion, poison
poosodie, sheep's-head broth
poutch, pocket
pouther, powder
pow(e), head
powt, chick
pree, try, taste
preen, *prin*, pin
preis, press, crowd
prenecod, pincushion (euphemism)
prunye, preen
put, thrust

quair, book
quean, quine, girl
quech, drinking-vessel
quha, who
quhairfoir, wherefor
quhat, what
quhile, quhyle, while
quhillilillie, penis
quhilk, which
quhome, whom
quhyte, white

rad, afraid
radgie, lustful
raep, rope
raid, ride
rair, roar
raik, hurry
ragment, catalogue
rak, crack
rame, roar
randy, lusty (woman)
rap, beat
rauch, proud
raucht, reached
rede, red; stark; council
reek, reik, smoke, steam
reid, red; council
reifery, robbery
reithe, ardent
remeid, remedy
responsaill, answer to prayer
rew, have pity
rift, belch
rigging, back
rigwoodie, withered
rise, brushwood
rive, rend
rode, rood, cross
roel, copulate
roif, ease
rossignel, nightingale
roun, rown, whisper
roup, auction
roust, complaint
rousty, rusty; spiritless
rowt, howl
ruffill, ruffling, bruising

runklet, wrinkled
rusing, boasting
ryce, branch
ryp(e), search, rake

sair, sore
sairy, sary, sorry
sakless, innocent
salat, slight service (lit. salad)
sanna, shall not
sanyne, signing with the cross
sark, shirt
saw, speech
scaith, skaith, wound, injury, wrong, harm
scart, scratch
scaul, scold
schaiffyne, shaven
schalk, churl
s(c)hank, leg
schaw, grove
schene, beautiful
schevill, wry, twisted
schore, fear
schrowd, dress
schup, shaped, undertook
schyre, sheer
scove, glide
scraich, skreigh, screetch
scrieve, write
scrimply, scarcely, barely
scoup, leap
scunner, (feel) disgust
scutarde, beshitten
seam, semen
seenil, seldom
sege, talk
semblit, assembled
semely, charmer
sensyne, since then
sew, sue
seyndill, seldom
shaest, chase
sharn, dung
shauchle, shamble
shaws, bushes
shent, undone
sic(can), such

sich, sigh
sicna, such a
sic thrums, ravelled loose threads
siller, money
skair, skare, share
skarth, cormorant
skeeg about, rhythmic strokes
sker, frightened
skirl, shriek
sklender, slender, skinny
skoit, peep
skouk, skulk
skrucken, shrunken
skyre, glitter
skyte, quick flight
slack, hollow
slawsy, ? slowcoach
slee, sly; skilful
slocken, slokyn, slake
slug, blouse
slummocked, lolling, sprawled
smake, feebly ingratiating
smeddum, courage
smit, infect
smolet, ? grimace
smool, steal away
smoor, smother
smy, wretch
sneck, snick, latch
snell, keen, bitter
snicher, snigger
snod, tidy, snug
snorled, entangled
sonsie, comely
sooth, south, truth
souter, cobbler
sowk(lar), suck(ler)
spane, spean, wean
spankie, spirited
speir, ask, enquire, enquiry
splairgin, splattering
spreit, spirit
spunk, match
spynist, blown (of a flower)
staig, stalk
stang, sting (penis)
stap, a dish made with fish and fish livers
stark, strong, hardy, stiff, rigid

steir, star; stir
stell, fix
storkyn, stiffen
stot, young bullock
stoup, flagon
stour, dust, muck
straik, stroke
stramash, din
strand, shoreline
strath, valley
straucht(ly), straight(away)
stron, headland
stumpie, worn quill pen (euphemism)
stunyst, astonished
styll, plight
sugsome, delay
sunkots, something, provision of some kind
sussy, trouble
swack, sturdy
swarf, swoon
swalme, swollen
swanquhit, swan-white
swat, sweated
swee, sway
sweer, sweir, reluctant
swerf, faint
swive, swyve, copulate
swonne, swoon
swyre, valley; glad
syde, at large
syle, mislead
syne, then
syte, grief
sytt, grieve

taen, tane, taken
taigle, ravel
tail-tree, penis
tak tent, take heed
talla, tallow (candle)
t'ane, the one
taper, slender
taz, whip
teen, vexatious
terne, fierce
teuchan, stuffed calf-skin
thae, thai, those

theekit, thatched
thegither, together
the morn, to-morrow
Thief, the Devil
thir, those
thirlage, bondage
thole, endure, suffer
thoom, thumb
tho(u)cht, thought; although
thra, boldly
thrang, crowd(ed)
thraw, twist
thrawe, while, time
tickle, rousingly
ticht, tight, shapely
tiend, tax, due
tine, tint, lose, lost
tirl, strip
tirlie-whirlie, pudenda
Tir-nan-Og, Land of Youth
t'ither, the other
tittie, young girl, sister
tod, fox
todlit, played
toed, scold
toetak, notorious person
toom, tuim, empty
towdie, pudenda
trane, entice
trattillis, prattle
trawe, trick
tribbill, treble
truff, steal
trogger, pedlar
trollie-lolly, penis
turtor, turtle-dove
twa(fauld), two(fold)
twin'd, parted

unco, odd, strange, very
unco-guid, all too respectable
unfullyeit, unspoiled
unstecht, unsurfeited
upwith, test
unyoun, onion

vailye quod vailye, come what may
vauntie, vain, proud

venust, charming
vieve, vivid
vogie, vain

wack, share
wad, pledge, forfeit; would; wed
waill, wale, choose
waly, fine, ample
wallidrag, weakling
wame, belly
wan, won
wanrife, unhappy
wariand, cursing
waris, dealt, spent
warp, utter
warssle, wrestle
wat, know
wauchied, enfeebled
waucht, drink
waukrife, wakening
waulis, genitals
waur, worse; surpass
wawlie, choice
wean, child
weel, well
weird, fate
wedis, clothes
wend, went, thought, believed
whatreck, fornication
whaul, whale
wheesht, hush
whinge, whine
whissle o my groat, a losing game
whummle, overturn
widdreme, confusion
wight, strong, stout; creature, fellow
wimble bore, gimlet crack
winnock, window
wir, our
wis, us
wlonkes, beauties
wobat, caterpillar
wodbind, woodbine
wod(de), wud, mad
wolroun, boar
wosp, straw stopper
wowf, wolf
wreuch, wretched

wrokin, avenged

wun, win

wynd, lane

wyte, blame

yaip, ardent

yerth, *yirth*, earth

yestreen, *yistrene*, yesterday

yett, gate

yoldin, soft

yowe, ewe

yuke, itch

Indexes

Index of First Lines

Index of Authors and Titles